Cook's Corner

Mug Cakes

igloobooks

igloobooks

Published in 2018
by Igloo Books Ltd
Cottage Farm
Sywell
NN6 0BJ
www.igloobooks.com

Cover image: © iStock / Getty Images

STA002 0218
2 4 6 8 10 9 7 5 3 1
ISBN: 978-1-78810-188-2

Cover designed by Nicholas Gage
Interiors designed by Simon Parker
Edited by Jasmin Peppiatt

Printed and manufactured in China

Cook's Corner

Mug Cakes

Contents

Cook's Corner

Mug Cakes

Classic mug cakes

Lemon drizzle

MAKES: 1 | PREP TIME: 15 MINUTES | COOKING TIME: 12 MINUTES, 30 SECONDS

INGREDIENTS

30 g / 1 oz butter

30 g / 1 oz caster (superfine) sugar

1 medium egg

30 g / 1 oz self-raising flour

1 tbsp milk

lemon slice to decorate

FOR THE SYRUP

1 tbsp caster (superfine) sugar

1 tbsp boiling water

zest and juice of half a lemon

METHOD

1. Preheat the oven to 180°C (160°C fan) / 425F / gas 4.

2. In a mug, make the syrup by combining the caster sugar with the boiling water. Stir in half of the lemon juice and cook in the centre of the microwave for 30 seconds. Allow to cool.

3. In a clean mug, mix the butter and sugar. Add the egg and stir until well mixed.

4. Gradually stir in the flour, then add the milk and mix well. Stir in the zest and remaining lemon juice.

5. Place the mug in the centre of the oven and cook for 10-12 minutes until well risen or until a skewer inserted in the centre comes out clean. Pour the lemon syrup over the cake whilst it is still warm.

6. Decorate with a lemon slice and serve.

Marzipan indulgence

MAKES: 2 | PREP TIME: 15 MINUTES | COOKING TIME: 1 MINUTE, 30 SECONDS

INGREDIENTS

55 g / 2 oz / ¼ cup butter, softened

55 g / 2 oz / 2 oz / ¼ cup caster (superfine) sugar

1 large egg

½ tsp almond extract

55 g / 2 oz / ⅓ cup self-raising flour, sifted

1 tbsp marzipan, cut into small chunks

TO DECORATE

1 small block of marzipan

icing (confectioner's) sugar for dusting

METHOD

1. Beat the butter and sugar together in a mug until pale and smooth.

2. Break the egg into a second mug and add the almond extract. Beat gently with a fork, then gradually stir the egg into the butter mixture.

3. Fold in the flour and marzipan chunks then spoon half of the mixture into the mug you used to beat the egg and level the tops.

4. Transfer the mugs to a microwave and cook on full power for 1 ½ minutes. Test the cakes by inserting a skewer into the centre – if it comes out clean, they're ready. If not, return to the microwave for 15 seconds and test again. Leave the cakes to cool completely.

5. Roll out the marzipan on a lightly dusted surface until it is approximately ½ cm (¼ in) thick, then cut out two circles to match the size of the mug tops. Top each cake with a marzipan circle.

6. Roll the remaining marzipan into balls and toast for a few seconds with a kitchen blow torch until lightly browned. Arrange the balls around the mug tops.

7. Dust with icing sugar and serve.

Chocolate soufflés

MAKES: 2 | PREP TIME: 10 MINUTES | COOKING TIME: 1 MINUTE, 30 SECONDS

INGREDIENTS

55 g / 2 oz / ¼ cup butter, softened

55 g / 2 oz / ¼ cup caster (superfine) sugar

1 large egg

55 g / 2 oz / ⅓ cup self-raising flour, sifted

2 tbsp unsweetened cocoa powder, plus extra for sprinkling

icing (confectioner's) sugar, for dusting

METHOD

1. Beat the butter and sugar together in a mug until pale and smooth.

2. Break the egg into a second mug and beat gently with a fork, then gradually stir the egg into the butter mixture.

3. Fold in the flour and cocoa powder, then spoon half of the mixture into the mug you used to beat the egg and level the tops.

4. Transfer the mugs to a microwave and cook on full power for 1 minute, 30 seconds. Test the cakes by inserting a skewer into the centre – if it comes out clean, they are ready. If not, return to the microwave for 15 seconds and test again.

5. Leave to rest for 1 minute, then dust the tops lightly with cocoa and icing sugar.

6. Delicious served with hot chocolate sauce (see Toppings chapter).

Sprinkles galore

MAKES: 2 | PREP TIME: 5 MINUTES | COOKING TIME: 1 MINUTE, 30 SECON

INGREDIENTS

50 g / 1 ¾ oz / ⅓ cup self-raising flour

50 g / 1 ¾ oz / ¼ cup caster (superfine) sugar

1 egg, beaten

2 tbsp milk

2 tbsp sunflower oil

½ tsp vanilla essence

2 tbsp sugar sprinkles

250 ml / 9 fl. oz / 1 cup double (heavy) cream

METHOD

1. Combine the flour and sugar in a mixing bowl. Add the egg and mix through as much as possible.

2. Add the milk, oil and vanilla essence and whisk to form a batter. Stir half the sprinkles through the batter before dividing between two mugs.

3. Transfer to a microwave and cook on full power for 1 minute, 30 seconds until risen and firm to the touch. Set aside to cool.

4. Whip the cream until it holds its shape and pipe onto the cakes before scattering over the remaining sprinkles.

Simply chocolate

MAKES: 1 | PREP TIME: 5 MINUTES | COOKING TIME: 1 MINUTE, 30 SECONDS

INGREDIENTS

40 g / 1 ½ oz / ¼ cup self-raising flour

40 g / 1 ½ oz / ¼ cup caster (superfine) sugar

20 g / ¾ oz cocoa powder

1 medium egg

2 tbsp milk

2 tbsp vegetable oil

1 tbsp chocolate chips

1 tsp icing (confectioner's) sugar

METHOD

1. Mix the flour, sugar and cocoa in a large mug.

2. Add the egg and thoroughly mix.

3. Combine the milk and oil in another mug, add to the batter and stir.

4. Fold in the chocolate chips.

5. Place the mug in the centre of the microwave and cook for 1 ½ minutes on full power.

6. Check the cake by placing a skewer into the centre of the cake; it should come out clean when fully cooked.

7. Sprinkle with icing sugar and serve.

15

Classic cherry

MAKES: 1 | PREP TIME: 5 MINUTES | COOKING TIME: 1 MINUTE, 30 SECONDS

INGREDIENTS

30 g / 1 oz butter

30 g / 1 oz caster (superfine) sugar

1 medium egg

30 g / 1 oz self-raising flour

1 tbsp milk

2 tbsp glacé cherries, halved

METHOD

1. Mix the butter and sugar in a large mug.

2. Add the egg and stir until well mixed.

3. Gradually stir in the flour, then add the milk and mix well.

4. Fold in the cherries.

5. Place the mug in the centre of the microwave and cook for 1 ½ minutes until well risen or until a skewer inserted in the centre comes out clean.

Plain and simple

MAKES: 2 | PREP TIME: 5 MINUTES | COOKING TIME: 1 MINUTE, 30 SECONDS

INGREDIENTS

55 g / 2 oz / ¼ cup butter, softened

55 g / 2 oz / ¼ cup caster (superfine) sugar

1 large egg

55 g / 2 oz / ⅓ cup self-raising flour, sifted

METHOD

1. Beat the butter and sugar together in a mug until pale and smooth.

2. Break the egg into a second mug and beat it gently, then gradually stir into the mixture.

3. Fold in the flour, then divide the mixture between the two mugs and level the tops.

4. Transfer to a microwave and cook for 1 ½ minutes on full power. Check the cake by placing a skewer into the centre of the cake; it should come out clean when fully cooked.

5. Leave the cakes to cool for 5 minutes. Serve on their own or with a delicious topping (see Toppings chapter).

Lemon curd

MAKES: 2 | PREP TIME: 20 MINUTES | COOKING TIME: 1 MINUTE, 30 SECONDS

INGREDIENTS

55 g / 2 oz / ¼ cup butter, softened

55 g / 2 oz / ¼ cup caster (superfine) sugar

1 lemon, zest finely grated

1 large egg

55 g / 2 oz / ⅓ cup self-raising flour, sifted

2 tbsp lemon curd

TO DECORATE

1 tsp lemon juice

55 g / 2 oz / ½ cup icing (confectioner's) sugar

METHOD

1. Beat the butter, sugar and lemon zest together in a mug until pale and smooth.

2. Break the egg into a second mug and beat gently, then gradually stir into the mixture.

3. Fold in the flour, followed by the lemon curd, then divide the mixture between the two mugs.

4. Transfer to a microwave and cook on full power for 1 ½ minutes or until a skewer inserted comes out clean.

5. Leave the cakes to cool for 10 minutes while you make the icing. Stir the lemon juice into the icing sugar a few drops at a time until thick but pourable. Drizzle over the cakes and serve.

Creamy coconut

MAKES: 1 | PREP TIME: 5 MINUTES | COOKING TIME: 1 MINUTE, 30 SECONDS

INGREDIENTS

30 g / 1 oz butter

30 g / 1 oz caster (superfine) sugar

1 medium egg

30 g / 1 oz self-raising flour

1 tbsp milk

1 tbsp desiccated coconut

TO SERVE

1 scoop of coconut ice cream

1 tsp desiccated coconut

METHOD

1. Mix the butter and sugar in a large mug. Add the egg and stir until well mixed.

2. Gradually stir in the flour, then add the milk and combine together before folding in the coconut.

3. Place the mug in the centre of the microwave and cook for 1 ½ minutes until well risen or until a skewer inserted in the centre comes out clean.

4. Top with coconut ice cream, sprinkle with a little desiccated coconut and serve immediately.

19

Elegant vanilla

MAKES: 2 | PREP TIME: 15 MINUTES | COOKING TIME: 1 MINUTE, 30 SECONDS

INGREDIENTS

55 g / 2 oz / ¼ cup butter, softened

55 g / 2 oz / ¼ cup caster (superfine) sugar

1 large egg

½ tsp vanilla extract

55 g / 2 oz / ⅓ cup self-raising flour, sifted

TO DECORATE

30 g / 1 oz / ½ cup butter, softened

75 g / 2 ½ oz / ¾ cup icing (confectioner's) sugar,
plus extra for dusting

½ tsp vanilla extract

½ vanilla pod, split lengthways

METHOD

1. Beat the butter and sugar together in a mug until pale and smooth.

2. Break the egg into a second mug and add the vanilla extract. Beat gently with a fork, then gradually stir the egg into the butter mixture.

3. Fold in the flour and then spoon half of the mixture into the mug you used to beat the egg and level the tops.

4. Transfer the mugs to a microwave and cook on full power for 1 ½ minutes. Test the cakes by inserting a skewer into the centre – if it comes out clean, the cakes are ready. If not, return to the microwave for 15 seconds and test again. Leave to cool completely.

5. Beat the butter, icing sugar and vanilla extract together until pale and well whipped, adding a few drops of hot water if the mixture is too stiff.

6. Spoon the buttercream into a piping bag fitted with a large star nozzle and pipe a big swirl on top of each cake.

7. Scrape the seeds out of the vanilla pod and dot them on top of the buttercream.

Strawberry and custard

MAKES: 2 | PREP TIME: 5 MINUTES | COOKING TIME: 2 MINUTES

INGREDIENTS

55 g / 2 oz / ¼ cup butter, softened

55 g / 2 oz / ¼ cup caster (superfine) sugar

1 large egg, beaten

55 g / 2 oz / ⅓ cup self-raising flour

2 tbsp milk

50 g / 1 ¾ oz / ½ cup strawberries

100 ml / 3 ½ fl. oz / ½ cup custard

METHOD

1. In a mixing bowl, beat the butter and sugar together until pale and smooth. Add the egg and mix through.

2. Sift the flour into the bowl and fold through, adding the milk to form a batter.

3. Roughly chop the strawberries and fold into the batter before spooning into two mugs.

4. Transfer the mugs to a microwave and cook on full power for 1 ½ minutes or until a skewer inserted comes out clean. Remove the cakes from the microwave and set aside.

5. Place the custard into a microwave proof bowl and heat in the microwave for 30 seconds on full until hot. Pour over the cakes and serve.

Toffee coffee

MAKES: 2 | PREP TIME: 20 MINUTES | COOKING TIME: 2 MINUTES, 15 SECONDS

INGREDIENTS

8 medjool dates, stoned and chopped

pinch bicarbonate of (baking) soda

55 g / 2 oz / ¼ cup butter, softened

55 g / 2 oz / ¼ cup dark muscovado sugar

55 g / 2 oz / ⅓ cup self-raising flour, sifted

1 tsp instant espresso powder

1 large egg, beaten

TO DECORATE

30 g / 1 oz / ½ cup butter, softened

75 g / 2 ½ oz / ¾ cup icing (confectioner's) sugar

½ tsp instant espresso powder

1 tsp black treacle

METHOD

1. Put the chopped dates in a mug with the bicarbonate of soda and 3 tablespoons of water. Microwave for 45 seconds.

2. Add the butter and stir until melted, then beat in the rest of the ingredients. Divide the mixture between two mugs and level.

3. Transfer the mugs to a microwave and cook on full power for 1 ½ minutes or until a skewer inserted comes out clean. Leave to cool completely.

4. Beat the decoration ingredients together until pale and well whipped, adding a few drops of hot water if the mixture is too stiff.

5. Pipe a swirl of the buttercream onto each cake using a piping bag fitted with a large star nozzle and serve.

Treacle and apple

MAKES: 2 | PREP TIME: 10 MINUTES | COOKING TIME: 5 MINUTES

INGREDIENTS

75 g / 2 ½ oz / ⅓ cup unsalted butter, softened

55 g / 2 oz / ¼ cup caster (superfine) sugar

1 large egg, beaten

55 g / 2 oz / ⅓ cup self-raising flour

2 tbsp apple sauce

2 tbsp golden syrup

2 tbsp salted butter

2 tbsp soft brown sugar

METHOD

1. In a mixing bowl, beat three quarters of the butter and the sugar together until pale and smooth. Add the egg to the bowl and mix through.

2. Sift the flour into the bowl and fold through half the apple sauce and syrup to form a batter. Divide between the two mugs and level the surface.

3. Transfer the mugs to a microwave and cook on full power for 1 ½ minutes or until a skewer inserted comes out clean. Remove from the microwave and leave to cool.

4. Melt the remaining butter in a saucepan with the remaining apple sauce, golden syrup and the brown sugar. Mix until melted and bubbling into a thick caramel, then leave to cook for 2-3 minutes.

5. Remove from the heat to cool a little before serving over the cakes.

Black Forest lava

MAKES: 2 | PREP TIME: 5 MINUTES | COOKING TIME: 1 MINUTE, 30 SECONDS

INGREDIENTS

2 tbsp black cherry jam (jelly)

55 g / 2 oz / ⅓ cup self-raising flour

55 g / 2 oz / ¼ cup caster (superfine) sugar

1 tbsp cocoa

55 g / 2 oz / ¼ cup butter, melted

2 tbsp milk

1 large egg, beaten

30 g / 1 oz dark chocolate chunks

METHOD

1. Spoon the jam into the bottom of two mugs.

2. Combine the flour, sugar and cocoa in a mixing bowl. Add the butter, milk and egg and whisk to form a batter.

3. Pour the batter into the mugs on top of the jam, then push the chocolate chunks into the centre of the cakes just below the surface of the batter.

4. Place into a microwave and cook on full for 1 ½ minutes or until the surface is just about set.

5. Remove and serve warm.

Vegan pumpkin with spice

MAKES: 4 | PREP TIME: 10 MINUTES | COOKING TIME: 45 SECONDS

INGREDIENTS

50 ml / 1 ¾ oz / ¼ cup maple syrup

50 ml / 1 ¾ oz / ¼ cup soya milk

2 tbsp sunflower oil

50 ml / 1 ¾ fl. oz / ¼ cup canned pumpkin purée

75 g / 2 ½ oz / ½ cup self-raising flour, sifted

½ tsp pumpkin pie spice mix, plus extra
for sprinkling

METHOD

1. Beat the maple syrup, milk, oil and pumpkin
   purée together in a large mug until pale
   and smooth.

2. Fold in the flour and pumpkin pie spice, then
   divide the mixture between four greased
   espresso cups and level the tops.

3. Transfer the cups to a microwave and cook on
   full power for 45 seconds. Test the cakes by
   inserting a skewer into the centre – if it comes
   out clean, they're ready. If not, return to the
   microwave for 10 seconds and test again.

4. Sprinkle with a little extra pie spice and serve
   warm or at room temperature.

Confetti sprinkles

MAKES: 2 | PREP TIME: 15 MINUTES | COOKING TIME: 1 MINUTE, 30 SECONDS

INGREDIENTS

55 g / 2 oz / ¼ cup butter, softened

55 g / 2 oz / ¼ cup light muscovado sugar

1 large egg

½ tsp vanilla extract

55 g / 2 oz / ⅓ cup self-raising flour, sifted

1 tbsp heart-shaped sugar confetti

METHOD

1. Beat the butter and sugar together in a mug until pale and smooth.

2. Break the egg into a second mug and add the vanilla extract. Beat gently with a fork, then gradually stir the egg into the butter mixture.

3. Fold in the flour, then divide between the two mugs and level the tops.

4. Transfer the mugs to a microwave and cook on full power for 1 ½ minutes or until a skewer inserted comes out clean. If not, return to the microwave for 15 seconds and test again.

5. Leave the cakes to cool for 5 minutes before serving with a sprinkle of sugar confetti.

Victoria sponge

MAKES: 1 | PREP TIME: 5 MINUTES | COOKING TIME: 1 MINUTE, 30 SECONDS

INGREDIENTS

30 g / 1 oz butter

30 g / 1 oz caster (superfine) sugar

1 medium egg

30 g / 1 oz self-raising flour

1 tbsp milk

1 tsp vanilla extract

1 tbsp strawberry jam (jelly), sieved

TO DECORATE

1 tsp caster (superfine) sugar

fresh strawberries

METHOD

1. Mix the butter and sugar in a large mug.
   Add the egg and stir until well mixed.

2. Gradually stir in the flour and add the milk
   and vanilla extract, mixing well.

3. Drop in the strawberry jam and allow to sink
   into the mixture without stirring.

4. Place the mug in the centre of the microwave
   and cook for 1 ½ minutes until well risen or
   until a skewer inserted in the centre comes
   out clean.

5. Sprinkle caster sugar on top and garnish
   with fresh strawberries.

31

Honey and lemon

MAKES: 2 | PREP TIME: 20 MINUTES | COOKING TIME: 1 MINUTE, 30 SECONDS

INGREDIENTS

55 g / 2 oz / ¼ cup butter, softened

55 g / 2 oz / ¼ cup caster (superfine) sugar

1 large egg

2 tbsp runny honey

2 tbsp lemon juice

55 g / 2 oz / ⅓ cup self-raising flour, sifted

½ unwaxed lemon, zested

TO DECORATE

30 g / 1 oz / ½ cup butter, softened

75 g / 2 ½ oz / ¾ cup icing (confectioner's) sugar

2 tbsp runny honey, plus a little extra for drizzling

½ tsp lemon extract

2 thick slices of unwaxed lemon

METHOD

1. Beat the butter and sugar together in a mug until pale and silky.

2. Break the egg into a second mug and add the runny honey and lemon juice. Beat gently with a fork, then gradually stir the egg into the butter mixture.

3. Fold in the flour and lemon zest, then spoon half of the mixture into the mug you used to beat the egg and level the tops.

4. Transfer the mugs to a microwave and cook on full power for 1 ½ minutes. Test the cakes by inserting a skewer into the centre – if it comes out clean, they're ready. If not, return to the microwave for 20 seconds and test again. Leave the cakes to cool completely.

5. Beat the butter, icing sugar, honey and lemon extract together until pale and well whipped, adding a few drops of hot water if the mixture is too stiff.

6. Spread the buttercream evenly on top of the cakes with a palette knife.

7. Top each cake with a slice of lemon drizzled with a little honey and serve.

Classic carrot

MAKES: 2 | PREP TIME: 15 MINUTES | COOKING TIME: 4 MINUTES

INGREDIENTS

60 g / 2 oz / ¼ cup self-raising flour

30 g / 1 oz brown sugar

a pinch of salt

¼ tsp ground cinnamon, plus extra for sprinkling

2 tbsp vegetable oil

1 medium egg

1 tbsp milk

30 g / 1 oz carrot, finely grated

FOR THE FROSTING

30 g / 1 oz cream cheese

30 g / 1 oz icing (confectioner's) sugar

METHOD

1. Mix the dry ingredients in a bowl. In a second bowl, mix the wet ingredients and carrot together.

2. Combine the two mixtures and divide between two mugs.

3. Place one of the mugs in the centre of the microwave and cook for 2 minutes. Check the cake after 1 ½ minutes by placing a skewer in the centre of the mug. If the skewer comes out clean, the cake is ready. Repeat with the second mug. Allow to cool.

4. To make the frosting, mix the cream cheese with the icing sugar.

5. Top the cooled carrot cakes with the frosting and dust with a little cinnamon before serving.

35

Coffee and walnut

MAKES: 2 | PREP TIME: 15 MINUTES | COOKING TIME: 1 MINUTE, 30 SECONDS

INGREDIENTS

55 g / 2 oz / ¼ cup butter, softened

55 g / 2 oz / ¼ cup caster (superfine) sugar

1 large egg

55 g / 2 oz / ⅓ cup self-raising flour, sifted

1 tsp instant espresso powder or 1 tsp coffee essence

1 tbsp cocoa powder

1 tbsp walnuts, finely chopped

TO DECORATE

30 g / 1 oz / ½ cup butter, softened

75 g / 2 ½ oz / ¾ cup icing (confectioner's) sugar

½ tsp instant espresso powder
or 1 tsp coffee essence

1 tbsp walnuts, finely chopped

4 chocolate coffee beans

METHOD

1. Beat the butter and sugar together in a mug until pale and smooth.

2. Break the egg into a second mug and beat gently with a fork, then gradually stir the egg into the butter mixture.

3. Fold in the flour, espresso powder or coffee essence and cocoa powder, then stir through the chopped walnut pieces. Spoon half of the mixture into the mug you used to beat the egg and level the tops.

4. Transfer the mugs to a microwave and cook on full power for 1 ½ minutes. Test the cakes by inserting a skewer into the centre – if it comes out clean, they're ready. If not, return to the microwave for 15 seconds and test again. Leave the cakes to cool completely.

5. Beat the butter, icing sugar and espresso powder or coffee essence together until pale and well whipped, adding a few drops of hot water if the mixture is too stiff.

6. Use a piping bag with a large star nozzle to pipe buttercream onto the cakes in a large swirl, decorate with chopped walnuts and chocolate coffee beans.

Egg-free strawberry classic

MAKES: 2 | PREP TIME: 10 MINUTES | COOKING TIME: 1 MINUTE, 30 SECONDS

INGREDIENTS

55 g / 2 oz / ¼ cup butter, softened

55 g / 2 oz / ¼ cup caster (superfine) sugar

2 tbsp Greek yogurt

1 tsp orange zest, finely grated

55 g / 2 oz / ⅓ cup self-raising flour, sifted

4 strawberries, halved

METHOD

1. Beat the butter and sugar together in a mug until pale and smooth, then beat in the yogurt and orange zest.

2. Fold in the flour, then spoon half of the mixture into a second mug. Push two strawberry halves down into each one and level the tops.

3. Transfer the mugs to a microwave and cook on full power for 1 ½ minutes. Test the cakes by inserting a skewer into the centre – if it comes out clean, they're ready. If not, return to the microwave for 15 seconds and test again.

4. Leave the cakes to cool for 5 minutes before serving, topped with the rest of the strawberries.

Gluten-free just chocolate

MAKES: 1 | PREP TIME: 5 MINUTES | COOKING TIME: 1 MINUTE

INGREDIENTS

1 ripe banana

2 tbsp cocoa powder

2 tbsp almond butter

1 tbsp milk

vanilla ice cream to serve

icing (confectioner's) sugar to dust

METHOD

1. Mash the banana together with the cocoa powder and almond butter to make a batter. Add the milk to loosen as required.

2. Pour the batter into a mug and transfer to a microwave. Cook on full power for 1 minute until a skewer inserted into the middle comes out clean. If not ready, then microwave for a further 15 seconds.

3. Serve the cake with a scoop of vanilla ice cream and dusted with icing sugar.

Chunky chocolate chip

MAKES: 1 | PREP TIME: 5 MINUTES | COOKING TIME: 1 MINUTE, 30 SECONDS

INGREDIENTS

30 g / 1 oz butter, softened

30 g / 1 oz caster (superfine) sugar

1 medium egg

30 g / 1 oz self-raising flour

1 tbsp milk

1 tbsp large chocolate chips

2 tsp orange marmalade

METHOD

1. Mix the butter and sugar in a large mug. Add the egg and stir until well mixed.

2. Gradually stir in the flour, then add the milk.

3. Fold in the chocolate chips and marmalade, reserving a little of each for the top.

4. Place the mug in the centre of the microwave and cook for 1 ½ minutes until well risen or until a skewer inserted in the centre comes out clean. Allow to cool, then drizzle a little marmalade and sprinkle the chocolate chips onto the top.

Pumpkin and ginger

MAKES: 2 | PREP TIME: 15 MINUTES | COOKING TIME: 1 MINUTE, 30 SECONDS

INGREDIENTS

50 ml / 1 ¾ oz / ¼ cup sunflower oil

55 g / 2 oz / ¼ cup light muscovado sugar

75 g / 2 ½ oz / ½ cup self-raising flour, sifted

½ tsp ground ginger

50 g / 1 ¾ oz / ½ cup pumpkin or butternut squash, finely grated

1 tsp cocoa powder

METHOD

1. Beat the oil and sugar together in a mug until pale and smooth. Fold in the flour and ground ginger, followed by the pumpkin. Divide the mixture between two mugs and level the tops.

2. Transfer the mugs to a microwave and cook on full power for 1 ½ minutes or until a skewer inserted into the centre comes out clean. If not, return to the microwave for 15 seconds and test again.

3. Sprinkle with a little cocoa powder and serve warm or at room temperature.

41

Sweet banana

MAKES: 2 | PREP TIME: 20 MINUTES | COOKING TIME: 16 MINUTES

INGREDIENTS

55 g / 2 oz / ¼ cup butter, softened

55 g / 2 oz / ¼ cup caster (superfine) sugar

1 large egg

½ tsp vanilla extract

55 g / 2 oz / ⅓ cup self-raising flour, sifted

1 large banana, lightly mashed

6–8 dried banana chips

icing (confectioner's) sugar for dusting

double (heavy) cream, to serve

METHOD

1. Preheat the oven to 160°C (140°C fan) /
    350F / gas 4.

2. Beat the butter and sugar together in an
    ovenproof mug until pale and smooth.

3. Break the egg into a second ovenproof mug
    with the vanilla extract. Beat gently then stir
    into the mixture.

4. Fold in the flour and mashed banana, then
    divide between two mugs and level the tops.

5. Top the cakes with banana chips, laying
    them flat onto the surface of the mixture.

6. Transfer the mugs to a baking tray and cook
    in the centre of the oven for 16 minutes until
    a skewer inserted into the centre comes out
    clean. If not, return to the oven for a couple
    of minutes and test again. Leave the cakes to
    cool a little and firm up.

7. Dust with icing sugar and serve warm with
    fresh cream.

Almond and jam

MAKES: 1 | PREP TIME: 5 MINUTES | COOKING TIME: 1 MINUTE, 30 SECONDS

INGREDIENTS

30 g / 1 oz butter, softened

30 g / 1 oz caster (superfine) sugar

1 medium egg

20 g / ¾ oz self-raising flour

2 tbsp ground almonds

1 tbsp milk

FOR THE FROSTING

1 tbsp icing (confectioner's) sugar

1 tbsp almonds

1 tsp strawberry jam (jelly)

METHOD

1. Mix the butter and sugar in a large mug, then stir in the egg until well mixed.

2. Gradually stir in the rest of the ingredients.

3. Place the mug in the centre of the microwave and cook for 1 ½ minutes until well risen or a skewer inserted into the centre comes out clean.

4. Place the icing sugar in a clean mug and gradually stir with 2 tsp of water.

5. Pour the icing over the cake, decorate with whole almonds and the jam and serve.

Chocolate hazelnut

MAKES: 2 | PREP TIME: 15 MINUTES | COOKING TIME: 1 MINUTE, 30 SECONDS

INGREDIENTS

55 g / 2 oz / ¼ cup butter, softened

55 g / 2 oz / ¼ cup caster (superfine) sugar

1 large egg

55 g / 2 oz / ⅓ cup self-raising flour, sifted

2 tbsp cocoa powder

1 tbsp hazelnuts (cobnuts), finely chopped

1 tbsp chocolate hazelnut (cobnut) spread

TO DECORATE

30 g / 1 oz / ½ cup butter, softened

75 g / 2 ½ oz / ¾ cup icing (confectioner's) sugar

2 tsp cocoa powder, plus a little extra for sprinkling

1 tbsp hazelnuts (cobnuts), finely chopped

METHOD

1. Beat the butter and sugar together in a mug until pale and smooth. Break the egg into a second mug and beat gently, then gradually stir into the mixture. Fold in the flour and cocoa powder. Stir through the chopped hazelnut pieces and chocolate spread. Divide between the two mugs and level the tops.

2. Transfer the mugs to a microwave and cook on full power for 1 ½ minutes until a skewer inserted into the centre comes out clean. If not, return to the microwave for 15 seconds and test again.

3. Leave the cakes to cool completely.

4. Make the decoration by beating the butter, icing sugar and cocoa powder until smooth and well whipped, adding a few drops of hot water if the mixture is too stiff.

5. Use a piping bag with a large star nozzle to pipe buttercream onto the cakes in a large swirl. Decorate with chopped hazelnuts and dust with cocoa powder.

Pumpkin pie

MAKES: 2 | PREP TIME: 5 MINUTES | COOKING TIME: 2 MINUTES

INGREDIENTS

55 g / 2 oz / ¼ cup butter, softened

55 g / 2 oz / ¼ cup caster (superfine) sugar

1 large egg, beaten

55 g / 2 oz / ⅓ cup self-raising flour

½ tsp cinnamon

½ tsp allspice

2 tbsp pumpkin purée

1 tbsp cream cheese

1 tbsp icing (confectioner's) sugar

METHOD

1. In a mixing bowl, beat the butter and sugar together until pale and smooth. Add the egg to the bowl and mix through.

2. Sift the flour and spices into the bowl and fold through the pumpkin purée to form a batter.

3. Spoon the mixture into two mugs and level off the surface.

4. Transfer to a microwave and cook on full power for 1 ½ minutes until a skewer inserted into the centre comes out clean. If not, return to the microwave for 15 seconds and test again.

5. Whisk together the cream cheese and icing sugar.

6. Remove the mugs from the microwave and leave to cool. Spoon the cream cheese icing on top and dust with a little more cinnamon or allspice.

Maple and pecan

MAKES: 2 | PREP TIME: 20 MINUTES | COOKING TIME: 1 MINUTE, 30 SECONDS

INGREDIENTS

55 g / 2 oz / ¼ cup butter, softened

55 g / 2 oz / ¼ cup caster (superfine) sugar

1 large egg

2 tsp natural maple syrup

55 g / 2 oz / ⅓ cup self-raising flour, sifted

8 pecan nuts, finely chopped

TO DECORATE

30 g / 1 oz / ½ cup butter, softened

5 g / 2 ½ oz / ¾ cup icing (confectioner's) sugar, plus extra for dusting

2 tsp natural maple syrup

10 pecan nuts, finely chopped

METHOD

1. Beat the butter and sugar together in a mug until pale and smooth.

2. Break the egg into a second mug and add the maple syrup. Beat together gently, then gradually stir into the butter mixture.

3. Fold in the flour and chopped pecan nuts, then divide equally between both mugs and level the tops.

4. Transfer the mugs to a microwave and cook on full power for 1 ½ minutes until a skewer inserted into the centre comes out clean. If not, return to the microwave for 15 seconds and test again. Leave the cakes to cool completely.

5. Make the topping by beating the butter, icing sugar and 1 teaspoon of maple syrup together until pale and well whipped, adding a few drops of hot water if the mixture is too stiff.

6. Spread the buttercream onto each cake and level with a palette knife. Dot a few drops of maple syrup around the edge of the buttercream.

7. Arrange the pecan nut quarters in a flower in the centre of each cake and dust with a little icing sugar.

Raspberry and vanilla

MAKES: 2 | PREP TIME: 20 MINUTES | COOKING TIME: 1 MINUTE, 30 SECONDS

INGREDIENTS

55 g / 2 oz / ¼ cup butter, softened

55 g / 2 oz / ¼ cup caster (superfine) sugar

1 large egg

55 g / 2 oz / ⅓ cup self-raising flour, sifted

6 fresh raspberries

TO DECORATE

30 g / 1 oz / ½ cup butter, softened

75 g / 2 ½ oz / ¾ cup icing (confectioner's) sugar,
plus extra for dusting

½ tsp vanilla extract

2 fresh raspberries

METHOD

1. Beat the butter and sugar together in a mug until pale and smooth.

2. Break the egg into a second mug. Beat gently with a fork, then gradually stir into the butter mixture.

3. Fold in the flour, then spoon half of the mixture into the mug you used to beat the egg. Push three raspberries down into the centre of each one and level the tops.

4. Transfer the mugs to a microwave and cook on full power for 1 ½ minutes until a skewer inserted into the centre comes out clean. If not, return to the microwave for 15 seconds and test again. Leave the cakes to cool completely.

5. Make a buttercream by beating the butter, icing sugar and vanilla extract together until pale and well whipped, adding a few drops of hot water if the mixture is too stiff.

6. Spoon the buttercream into a piping bag fitted with a large star nozzle and pipe a big swirl on top of each cake. Top each one with a raspberry and serve immediately.

Chocolate and peanut

MAKES: 2 | PREP TIME: 10 MINUTES | COOKING TIME: 1 MINUTE, 30 SECONDS

INGREDIENTS

50 g / 1 ¾ oz / ⅓ cup self-raising flour

50 g / 1 ¾ oz / ¼ cup caster (superfine) sugar

2 tbsp cocoa powder

1 egg, beaten

2 tbsp peanut butter

2 tbsp sunflower oil

METHOD

1. Combine the flour, sugar and cocoa powder in a mixing bowl and mix through the egg.

2. Add the peanut butter and oil and whisk to form a batter.

3. Divide the batter between two mugs and transfer to a microwave to cook on full power for 1 minute, 30 seconds until risen and a skewer inserted into the centre comes out clean.

4. Remove and set aside to cool.

54

Tangy ginger

MAKES: 1 | PREP TIME: 5 MINUTES | COOKING TIME: 1 MINUTE, 30 SECONDS

INGREDIENTS

30 g / 1 oz butter, softened

30 g / 1 oz caster (superfine) sugar

1 medium egg

30 g / 1 oz self-raising flour

½ tsp ground ginger

1 tbsp milk

1 tbsp ginger conserve

TO DECORATE

1 tbsp ginger conserve or candied ginger pieces

METHOD

1. Mix the butter and sugar in a large mug. Add the egg and stir until well mixed.

2. Gradually stir in the flour and ginger. Add the milk and mix well, then fold in the ginger conserve.

3. Place the mug in the centre of the microwave and cook for 1 ½ minutes until well risen or until a skewer inserted in the centre comes out clean.

4. Top with more ginger conserve or candied ginger to serve.

55

Cinnamon roll

MAKES: 1 | PREP TIME: 10 MINUTES | COOKING TIME: 2 MINUTES

INGREDIENTS

30 g / 1 oz self-raising flour

30 g / 1 oz caster (superfine) sugar

½ tsp cinnamon

a pinch of nutmeg

2 tbsp whole milk

2 tsp vegetable oil

2 tbsp brown sugar

2 tbsp butter

1 tbsp cream cheese

2 tbsp icing (confectioner's) sugar

METHOD

1. Mix the flour, caster sugar, half the cinnamon, nutmeg, milk and oil in a mixing bowl. Whisk until a batter forms.

2. Place the brown sugar, remaining cinnamon and half the butter into a microwavable bowl. Cook in the microwave for 30 seconds until the butter has melted, then stir to fully combine.

3. Spoon half the cake batter into a mug and then swirl half the cinnamon butter into this. Top with the remaining batter and then add another swirl.

4. Transfer the mug to a microwave and cook on full power for 1 ½ minutes until a skewer inserted into the centre comes out clean. Microwave for a further 15 seconds if not cooked. Set aside to cool.

5. Whisk together the remaining butter, cream cheese and icing sugar to make a topping. Spoon into a piping bag and pipe a swirl on top of the cake before serving. Lightly dust with cinnamon as desired.

Date and walnut

MAKES: 2 | PREP TIME: 15 MINUTES | COOKING TIME: 16 MINUTES

INGREDIENTS

55 g / 2 oz / ¼ cup butter, softened

55 g / 2 oz / ¼ cup caster (superfine) sugar

1 large egg

55 g / 2 oz / ⅓ cup self-raising flour, sifted

¼ tsp ground cinnamon

2 tsp walnuts, finely chopped

2–3 large dates, stoned and finely chopped

TO DECORATE

30 g / 1 oz / ½ cup butter, softened

75 g / 2 ½ oz / ¾ cup icing (confectioner's) sugar,
plus extra for dusting

½ tsp vanilla extract

2 large dates, stoned

4 walnut halves

METHOD

1. Preheat the oven to 160°C (140°C fan) / 350F / gas 4.

2. Beat the butter and sugar together in an ovenproof mug until pale and smooth.

3. Break the egg into a second ovenproof mug. Beat gently with a fork, then gradually stir the egg into the butter mixture.

4. Fold in the flour, ground cinnamon, chopped walnuts and dates, then spoon half of the mixture into the mug you used to beat the egg and level the tops.

5. Transfer the mugs to a baking tray and cook in the centre of the oven for 16 minutes. Test the cakes by inserting a skewer into the centre – if it comes out clean, they're ready. If not, return to the oven for a couple of minutes and test again. Leave the cakes to cool completely.

6. Make a buttercream by beating the butter, icing sugar and vanilla extract together until pale and smooth, adding a few drops of hot water if the mixture is too stiff.

7. Spoon the buttercream into a piping bag fitted with a large plain nozzle and pipe a pillow on top of each cake. Top with a date and two walnut halves, then dust with icing sugar to serve.

White chocolate

MAKES: 2 | PREP TIME: 20 MINUTES | COOKING TIME: 1 MINUTE, 30 SECONDS

INGREDIENTS

55 g / 2 oz / ¼ cup butter, softened

55 g / 2 oz / ¼ cup caster (superfine) sugar

1 large egg

55 g / 2 oz / ⅓ cup self-raising flour, sifted

1 tbsp white chocolate chunks

TO DECORATE

100 g / 3 ½ oz bar of white chocolate

2 white chocolate cigarillos

2 plain chocolate cigarillos

METHOD

1. Beat the butter and sugar together in a mug until pale and smooth.

2. Gently beat the egg into a second mug and stir into the mixture. Fold in the flour and white chocolate chunks, then divide between the two mugs and level the tops.

3. Transfer the mugs to a microwave and cook on full power for 1 ½ minutes or until a skewer inserted comes out clean. Leave the cakes to cool completely.

4. Melt the white chocolate, saving a couple of pieces for making shavings. Pour over each cake and allow to cool a little. As the chocolate begins to harden, stick two chocolate cigarillos into each cake.

5. Once set, make some chocolate shavings with the reserved white chocolate, sprinkle over the tops and serve.

Dairy-free love

MAKES: 2 | PREP TIME: 15 MINUTES | COOKING TIME: 1 MINUTE, 30 SECONDS

INGREDIENTS

55 g / 2 oz / ¼ cup dairy-free butter
(or spread), softened

55 g / 2 oz / ¼ cup light muscovado sugar

1 large egg

1 tsp orange zest, finely grated

55 g / 2 oz / ⅓ cup self-raising flour, sifted

2 tbsp heart-shaped sugar confetti

METHOD

1. Beat the dairy-free butter and sugar together in a mug until pale and smooth.

2. Break the egg into a second mug and add the orange zest. Beat gently with a fork, then gradually stir the into the butter mixture.

3. Fold in the flour and half the confetti, then spoon half of the mixture into the mug you used to beat the egg and level the tops. Sprinkle over the rest of the confetti.

4. Transfer the mugs to a microwave and cook on full power for 1 ½ minutes until a skewer inserted comes out clean. If not, return to the microwave for 15 seconds and test again.

5. Leave the cakes to cool for 5 minutes before serving.

Cinnamon and raisins

MAKES: 2 | PREP TIME: 20 MINUTES | COOKING TIME: 1 MINUTE, 30 SECONDS

INGREDIENTS

55 g / 2 oz / ¼ cup butter, softened

55 g / 2 oz / ¼ cup caster (superfine) sugar

1 large egg

55 g / 2 oz / ⅓ cup self-raising flour, sifted

1 tsp ground cinnamon

1 tbsp raisins

1 tbsp cinnamon sugar

1 cinnamon stick, halved

METHOD

1. Beat the butter and sugar together in a mug until pale and smooth.

2. Break the egg into a second mug and beat gently with a fork, then gradually stir into the butter mixture.

3. Fold in the flour and ground cinnamon, followed by the raisins, then spoon half of the mixture into the mug used to beat the egg and level the tops.

4. Transfer the mugs to a microwave and cook on full power for 1 ½ minutes until a skewer inserted into the centre comes out clean. If not, return to the microwave for 15 seconds and test again.

5. Sprinkle the top of the cakes with cinnamon sugar and brown them lightly under a hot grill. Serve warm or at room temperature, garnished with cinnamon stick halves.

Chocolate chunk

MAKES: 2 | PREP TIME: 15 MINUTES | COOKING TIME: 1 MINUTE, 30 SECONDS

INGREDIENTS

55 g / 2 oz / ¼ cup butter, softened

55 g / 2 oz / ¼ cup caster (superfine) sugar

1 large egg

55 g / 2 oz / ⅓ cup self-raising flour, sifted

2 tbsp unsweetened cocoa powder

30 g / 1 oz / ⅓ cup milk chocolate, chopped,
plus extra for grating over

METHOD

1. Beat the butter and sugar together in a mug until pale and smooth.

2. Break the egg into a second mug and beat gently with a fork, then gradually stir into the butter mixture.

3. Fold in the flour, cocoa powder and chopped chocolate, then spoon half of the mixture into the mug you used to beat the egg and level the tops.

4. Transfer the mugs to a microwave and cook on full power for 1 ½ minutes until a skewer inserted into the centre comes out clean. If not, return to the microwave for 15 seconds and test again.

5. Leave to cool for 5 minutes, then grate over a little more chocolate.

6. Delicious served with vanilla custard (see Toppings chapter).

Cook's Corner

Mug Cakes

Fruity mug cakes

Apple crumbles

MAKES: 2 | PREP TIME: 30 MINUTES | COOKING TIME: 1 MINUTE, 30 SECONDS

INGREDIENTS

55 g / 2 oz / ¼ cup butter, softened

55 g / 2 oz / ¼ cup caster (superfine) sugar

1 large egg

55 g / 2 oz / ⅓ cup self-raising flour, sifted

½ tsp ground cinnamon

1 small apple, peeled, cored and diced, 4 slices
reserved to garnish

1 handful of raisins

FOR THE CRUMBLE

2 tbsp butter, diced

4 tbsp plain (all-purpose) flour

2 tbsp soft light brown sugar

METHOD

1. Beat the butter and sugar together in a mug
until pale and smooth.

2. Break the egg into a second mug and beat
gently with a fork, then gradually stir into
the butter mixture.

3. Fold in the flour and ground cinnamon,
followed by the apple and raisins, then
spoon half of the mixture into the mug you
used to beat the egg and level the tops.

4. To make the crumble topping, rub the butter
into the flour, then stir in the sugar. Sprinkle
it over the cake mixture in the mugs.

5. Transfer the mugs to a microwave and cook
on full power for 1 ½ minutes until a skewer
inserted into the centre comes out clean.
If not, return to the microwave for 15 seconds
and test again.

6. Brown the crumble lightly under a hot grill
and serve warm or at room temperature,
topped with apple slices.

Mini fruit cakes

MAKES: 2 | PREP TIME: 20 MINUTES | COOKING TIME: 7 MINUTES

INGREDIENTS

55 g / 2 oz / ¼ cup butter, softened

55 g / 2 oz / ¼ cup dark muscovado sugar

1 large egg

1 tsp citrus peel, finely chopped

2 tsp raisins

55 g / 2 oz / ⅓ cup self-raising flour, sifted

TO DECORATE

6–8 tbsp caster (superfine) sugar

4–6 tbsp water

4 tbsp whole pistachios, shelled and unsalted

2 tbsp dried cranberries

16 hazelnuts (cobnuts), shelled

4 whole almonds

METHOD

1. Preheat the oven to 160°C (140°C fan) / 350F / gas 4. Beat the butter and sugar together in an ovenproof mug.

2. Break the egg into a second ovenproof mug. Beat with a fork, then gradually stir into the butter mixture.

3. Fold in the peel, raisins and flour, mixing to combine. Spoon half of the mixture into the mug you used to beat the egg and level the tops. Transfer the mugs to a baking tray and cook in the oven for 16 minutes. Leave the cakes to cool completely.

4. To decorate, mix the sugar with the water over a medium heat until it has dissolved into a thick syrup. Brush the syrup over the tops of the cooled cakes, then arrange the nuts and dried fruit across the cakes, ready to serve.

Rhubarb delight

MAKES: 2 | PREP TIME: 5 MINUTES | COOKING TIME: 2 MINUTES

INGREDIENTS

55 g / 2 oz / ¼ cup butter, softened

55 g / 2 oz / ¼ cup caster (superfine) sugar

1 large egg, beaten

55 g / 2 oz / ⅓ cup self-raising flour

2 tbsp milk

50 g / 1 ¾ oz / ½ cup rhubarb pieces in syrup

METHOD

1. In a mixing bowl, beat the butter and sugar together until pale and smooth. Add the egg and mix through until consistent.

2. Sift the flour into the bowl and fold through the milk and rhubarb in syrup to form a batter.

3. Spoon the mixture into two mugs and level off the surface.

4. Transfer the mugs to a microwave and cook on full power for 1 ½ minutes until a skewer inserted into the centre comes out clean. If not, return to the microwave for 15 seconds and test again.

5. Allow to cool a little before serving. Superb drizzled with fresh custard.

Raspberry swirl

MAKES: 1 | PREP TIME: 7 MINUTES | COOKING TIME: 1 MINUTE, 30 SECONDS

INGREDIENTS

30 g / 1 oz butter, softened

30 g / 1 oz caster (superfine) sugar

1 medium egg

30 g / 1 oz self-raising flour

1 tbsp milk

1 tbsp freeze-dried raspberry pieces

FOR THE FROSTING

10 g / ⅓ oz / 2 tbsp butter, softened

20 g / ¾ oz / ¼ cup icing (confectioner's) sugar

1 tbsp raspberry jam (jelly), sieved

METHOD

1. Mix the butter and sugar in a large mug. Add the egg and stir until well mixed. Gradually stir in the flour, then add the milk and mix well before stirring in the raspberries.

2. Place the mug in the centre of the microwave and cook for 1 ½ minutes until well risen or until a skewer inserted in the centre comes out clean.

3. To make the frosting, combine the butter and icing sugar and mix well. Gently fold in the raspberry jam, to create a swirl effect.

4. Use a star nozzle to pipe the frosting onto the cooled cake and sprinkle with more freeze-dried raspberry pieces, if desired, before serving.

75

Breakfast cakes

MAKES: 2 | PREP TIME: 20 MINUTES | COOKING TIME: 1 MINUTE, 30 SECONDS

INGREDIENTS

55 g / 2 oz / ¼ cup butter, softened

55 g / 2 oz / ¼ cup caster (superfine) sugar

1 large egg

55 g / 2 oz / ⅓ cup self-raising flour, sifted

1 tbsp raisins

1 tbsp apple juice

2 tbsp Greek yogurt

2 tbsp toasted oats

fresh fruit, to garnish

METHOD

1. Beat the butter and sugar together in a mug until pale and smooth.

2. Break the egg into a second mug and beat gently, then gradually stir into the butter mixture.

3. Fold in the flour, followed by the raisins and apple juice, then spoon half of the mixture into the mug you used to beat the egg and level the tops.

4. Transfer the mugs to a microwave and cook on full power for 1 ½ minutes and a skewer inserted into the centre comes out clean. If not, return to the microwave for 15 seconds and test again.

5. Leave to cool for 5 minutes, then top with yogurt, toasted oats and fresh fruit.

Blueberry muffins

MAKES: 2 | PREP TIME: 5 MINUTES | COOKING TIME: 1 MINUTE, 30 SECONDS

INGREDIENTS

50 g / 1 ¾ oz / ½ cup self-raising flour

50 g / 1 ¾ oz / ½ cup caster (superfine) sugar

2 tbsp milk

1 egg, beaten

2 tbsp butter, melted

½ tsp vanilla extract

25 g / 1 oz / ¼ cup blueberries, washed

METHOD

1. Mix the flour and sugar together in a mixing bowl, then make a well in the centre.

2. Whisk together the milk, egg, butter and vanilla until frothy. Pour into the dry ingredients and mix just enough to combine. Fold the blueberries through the batter.

3. Spoon into two mugs and cook in a microwave on full power for 1 ½ minutes until a skewer inserted into the centre comes out clean. If not, return to the microwave for 15 seconds and test again.

4. Remove to cool before serving.

Piña colada

MAKES: 2 | PREP TIME: 5 MINUTES | COOKING TIME: 1 MINUTE, 30 SECONDS

INGREDIENTS

55 g / 2 oz / ¼ cup butter, softened

55 g / 2 oz / ¼ cup caster (superfine) sugar

1 large egg, beaten

55 g / 2 oz / ⅓ cup self-raising flour

4 pineapple rings

2 tbsp grated coconut

50 ml / 1 ¾ fl. oz / ¼ cup white rum

2 glacé cherries

METHOD

1. In a mixing bowl, beat the butter and sugar together until pale and smooth. Add the egg to the bowl and mix through, then sift the flour into the bowl and fold through to form a batter.

2. Chop two of the pineapple rings into pieces and fold through the cake batter along with the coconut.

3. Spoon the mixture into two mugs and level off the surface.

4. Transfer the mugs to a microwave and cook on full power for 1 ½ minutes until a skewer inserted into the centre comes out clean. If not, return to the microwave for 15 seconds and test again.

5. Remove the cakes from the microwave and pour over the rum so that it soaks into the sponge.

6. Place the remaining pineapple rings and the glacé cherries on top.

Passion fruit

MAKES: 1 | PREP TIME: 15 MINUTES | COOKING TIME: 2 MINUTES

INGREDIENTS

30 g / 1 oz butter, softened

30 g / 1 oz caster (superfine) sugar

1 medium egg

30 g / 1 oz self-raising flour

1 tbsp milk

1 tbsp white chocolate chips

seeds and flesh of ½ passion fruit

FOR THE FROSTING

20 g / ¾ oz / ¼ cup icing (confectioner's) sugar

10 g soft butter

1 tbsp grated white chocolate

METHOD

1. Mix the butter and sugar in a large mug and add the egg and stir until well mixed. Gradually stir in the flour, then mix in the milk until combined.

2. Stir in the chocolate chips and half of the passion fruit seeds.

3. Place the mug in the centre of the microwave and cook for 1 ½ minutes until well risen or until a skewer inserted in the centre comes out clean. Allow to cool.

4. To make the topping, combine the icing sugar and butter and mix until light and fluffy.

5. Melt the white chocolate for 20 seconds in the microwave.

6. Fold the melted white chocolate and remaining passion fruit into the frosting.

7. Spoon the frosting onto the top of the cake and serve.

Coconut and lime

MAKES: 2 | PREP TIME: 5 MINUTES | COOKING TIME: 1 MINUTE, 30 SECONDS

INGREDIENTS

55 g / 2 oz / ¼ cup butter, softened

55 g / 2 oz / ¼ cup caster (superfine) sugar

1 large egg

½ tsp lime extract

55 g / 2 oz / ⅓ cup self-raising flour, sifted

4 tsp desiccated coconut

TO DECORATE

50 g / 2 oz / ½ cup butter, softened

75 g / 2 ½ oz / ¾ cup icing (confectioner's) sugar

½ tsp lime extract

2 tsp dried coconut pieces

½ lime, zested

METHOD

1. Beat the butter and sugar together in a mug until pale and smooth.

2. Break the egg into a second mug and add the lime extract. Beat gently, then gradually stir into the butter mixture.

3. Fold in the flour and stir through the desiccated coconut, then spoon half of the mixture into the mug you used to beat the egg and level the tops.

4. Transfer the mugs to a microwave and cook on full power for 1 ½ minutes until a skewer inserted into the centre comes out clean. If not, return to the microwave for 15 seconds and test again. Leave the cakes to cool.

5. To decorate, beat the butter, icing sugar and lime extract together until creamy, adding a few drops of hot water if the mixture is too stiff. Spoon the buttercream onto the top of each cake and smooth into a dome with the back of a spoon.

6. Top with the dried coconut pieces and sprinkle with lime zest before serving.

Apricot cream

MAKES: 2 | PREP TIME: 15 MINUTES | COOKING TIME: 1 MINUTE, 30 SECONDS

INGREDIENTS

55 g / 2 oz / ¼ cup butter, softened

55 g / 2 oz / ¼ cup caster (superfine) sugar

1 large egg

55 g / 2 oz / ⅓ cup self-raising flour, sifted

4 canned apricot halves, finely diced

1 tbsp apricot jam (jelly)

TO DECORATE

30 g / 1 oz / ½ cup butter, softened

75 g / 2 ½ oz / ¾ cup icing (confectioner's) sugar, plus extra for dusting

½ tsp vanilla extract

6 canned apricot halves

METHOD

1. Beat the butter and sugar together in a mug until pale and smooth.

2. Break the egg into a second mug and beat gently, then gradually stir the egg into the butter mixture.

3. Fold in the flour, followed by the apricot pieces and jam, then spoon half of the mixture into the mug you used to beat the egg and level the tops.

4. Transfer the mugs to a microwave and cook on full power for 1 ½ minutes until a skewer inserted into the centre comes out clean. If not, return to the microwave for 15 seconds and test again. Leave the cakes to cool completely.

5. To decorate, beat the butter and icing sugar and vanilla extract together until pale and creamy.

6. Spoon the buttercream into a piping bag fitted with a large plain nozzle and pipe a ring round the edge of each cake.

7. Fill the centre of each buttercream ring with the apricot halves.

Strawberries and cream

MAKES: 2 | PREP TIME: 35 MINUTES | COOKING TIME: 2 MINUTES

INGREDIENTS

50 g / 1 ¾ oz / ½ cup fresh strawberries, chopped

100 g / 3 ½ oz / ½ cup caster (superfine) sugar

55 g / 2 oz / ¼ cup butter, softened

1 large egg, beaten

55 g / 2 oz / ⅓ cup self-raising flour

1 tbsp double (heavy) cream

1 tsp vanilla extract

METHOD

1. Place the chopped strawberries into a bowl and cover with half the sugar. Cover and leave to macerate for 30 minutes so that their juices have been released but they have not gone mushy.

2. Beat together the butter and remaining sugar in a bowl until pale and creamy. Mix the egg into the butter.

3. Sift the flour into the butter and fold through before adding the strawberry juice, cream and vanilla extract.

4. Divide between two large mugs and smooth off the surface. Transfer the mugs to a microwave and cook on full power for 2 minutes until a skewer inserted into the centre comes out clean. If not, return to the microwave for 15 seconds and test again

5. Serve the cakes either warm or cold with the macerated strawberries on top.

Vegan banana sponge

MAKES: 1 | PREP TIME: 10 MINUTES | COOKING TIME: 1 MINUTE, 30 SECONDS

INGREDIENTS

1 very ripe banana, ½ mashed, ½ sliced

2 tbsp soya milk

1 tbsp sunflower oil

¼ tsp vanilla extract

50 g / 1 ¾ oz / ⅓ cup self-raising flour

2 tbsp caster (superfine) sugar

METHOD

1. Whisk the mashed banana with the soya milk, oil and vanilla extract with a fork in a small mug. Add the flour and caster sugar and stir well, then level the surface.

2. Transfer the mug to a microwave and cook on full power for 1 ½ minutes until a skewer inserted into the centre comes out clean. If not, return to the microwave for 10 seconds and test again.

3. Leave to cool for 5 minutes, then top with the sliced banana and serve.

Vegan apple muffin

MAKES: 1 | PREP TIME: 15 MINUTES | COOKING TIME: 1 MINUTE

INGREDIENTS

2 tbsp dairy-free cream

2 tbsp coconut milk

½ tbsp sunflower oil

¼ lemon, juiced

50 g / 1 ¾ oz / ⅓ cup self-raising flour

2 tbsp caster (superfine) sugar

½ small eating apple, cored and chopped

2 tbsp icing (confectioner's) sugar

METHOD

1. Mix 1 tablespoon of the dairy-free cream with the coconut milk, oil and lemon juice in a mug. Add the flour and caster sugar and stir, then fold in the chopped apple.

2. Transfer the mug to a microwave and cook on full power for 1 minute until a skewer inserted into the centre comes out clean. If not, return to the microwave for 10 seconds and test again. Leave to cool for 5 minutes.

3. Mix the remaining tablespoon of dairy-free cream with the icing sugar and drizzle it over the top before serving.

Cocoa cranberry

MAKES: 2 | PREP TIME: 10 MINUTES | COOKING TIME: 2 MINUTES

INGREDIENTS

55 g / 2 oz / ¼ cup butter, softened

55 g / 2 oz / ¼ cup caster (superfine) sugar

1 large egg

55 g / 2 oz / ⅓ cup self-raising flour, sifted

2 tbsp unsweetened cocoa powder, plus extra
for sprinkling

1 tbsp dried cranberries

icing (confectioner's) sugar, for dusting

2 tsp cranberry jam (jelly)

METHOD

1. Beat the butter and sugar together in a small mug
until pale and smooth.

2. Break the egg into a second mug and beat gently,
then gradually stir into the butter mixture.

3. Fold in the flour, cocoa powder and dried
cranberries, then spoon half of the mixture into
the mug you used to beat the egg and level the tops.

4. Transfer the mugs to a microwave and cook on
full power for 1 ½ minutes until a skewer inserted
into the centre comes out clean. If not, return to
the microwave for 15 seconds and test again.
Leave to cool for 5 minutes.

5. Dust the tops lightly with icing sugar and add a
spoonful of cranberry jam to each one.

90

Blueberry custard

MAKES: 2 | PREP TIME: 10 MINUTES | COOKING TIME: 1 MINUTE, 30 SECONDS

INGREDIENTS

55 g / 2 oz / ¼ cup butter, softened

55 g / 2 oz / ¼ cup caster (superfine) sugar,
plus extra for sprinkling

30 g / 1 oz custard powder

75 ml / 2 ½ fl. oz / ⅓ cup whole milk

55 g / 2 oz / ⅓ cup self-raising flour, sifted

1 handful blueberries

METHOD

1. Beat the butter and sugar together in a mug
   until pale and smooth.
2. Whisk the custard powder and milk together
   in a second mug until smooth, then beat it into
   the butter mixture.
3. Fold in the flour and blueberries, then spoon
   half of the mixture into the mug you mixed
   the custard in and level the tops.
4. Transfer the mugs to a microwave and cook on
   full power for 1 ½ minutes until a skewer
   inserted into the centre comes out clean. If
   not, return to the microwave for 15 seconds
   and test again.
5. Leave the cakes to cool for 5 minutes before
   serving, sprinkled with caster sugar.

Pineapple and banana

MAKES: 2 | PREP TIME: 15 MINUTES | COOKING TIME: 1 MINUTE, 30 SECONDS

INGREDIENTS

55 g / 2 oz / ¼ cup butter, softened

55 g / 2 oz / ¼ cup caster (superfine) sugar

1 large egg

½ tsp vanilla extract

½ fresh banana, roughly mashed

2 tbsp canned pineapple chunks, drained and finely chopped

55 g / 2 oz / ⅓ cup self-raising flour, sifted

TO DECORATE

30 g / 1 oz / ½ cup butter, softened

75 g / 2 ½ oz / ¾ cup icing (confectioner's) sugar, plus extra for dusting

½ tsp vanilla extract

6 pieces of dried or candied pineapple

METHOD

1. Beat the butter and sugar together in a mug until pale and smooth.

2. Break the egg into a second mug and add the vanilla extract. Beat gently with a fork, then gradually stir into the butter mixture. Mix through the banana and pineapple pieces.

3. Fold in the flour, then divide the mixture between the two mugs.

4. Transfer the mugs to a microwave and cook on full power for 1 ½ minutes until a skewer inserted into the centre comes out clean. If not, return to the microwave for 15 seconds and test again. Leave to cool completely.

5. To decorate, beat the butter, icing sugar and vanilla extract together until pale and creamy, adding a few drops of hot water if the mixture is too stiff.

6. Spoon the buttercream into a piping bag fitted with a small plain nozzle and pipe teardrops around top of each cake.

7. Top each cake with a few pieces of dried or candied pineapple and dust with icing sugar to serve.

Fig and pear

MAKES: 2 | PREP TIME: 30 MINUTES | COOKING TIME: 16 MINUTES

INGREDIENTS

55 g / 2 oz / ¼ cup butter, softened

55 g / 2 oz / ¼ cup caster (superfine) sugar

1 large egg

1 ½ tsp sirop de figue

55 g / 2 oz / ⅓ cup self-raising flour, sifted

2 dried figs, finely chopped

2 canned pear halves, finely diced

TO DECORATE

icing (confectioner's) sugar for dusting

METHOD

1. Preheat the oven to 160°C (140°C fan) / 350F / gas 4. Beat the butter and sugar together in an ovenproof mug until pale and smooth.

2. Break the egg into a second ovenproof mug and add the sirop de figue. Beat gently, then gradually stir into the butter mixture.

3. Fold in the flour, chopped figs and diced pears, then divide the mixture between the two mugs and level the tops.

4. Transfer the mugs to a baking tray and cook in the centre of the oven for 16 minutes until a skewer inserted into the centre comes out clean. If not, return to the oven for a couple of minutes and test again. Leave the cakes to cool a little.

5. Dust each cake with a little icing sugar before serving warm.

6. Vanilla custard makes an ideal topping (see Toppings chapter).

Blackberry cheesecake

MAKES: 2 | PREP TIME: 20 MINUTES | COOKING TIME: 1 MINUTE, 30 SECONDS

INGREDIENTS

55 g / 2 oz / ¼ cup butter, softened

55 g / 2 oz / ¼ cup caster (superfine) sugar

1 large egg

55 g / 2 oz / ⅓ cup self-raising flour, sifted

2 tbsp fresh blackberries, chopped

TO DECORATE

250 ml / 9 fl. oz / 1 cup fresh whipping cream

2 tbsp icing (confectioner's) sugar, plus
extra for dusting

2 tbsp cream cheese

4–6 fresh blackberries

METHOD

1. Beat the butter and sugar together in a mug until pale and shiny.

2. Break the egg into a second mug. Beat gently, then gradually stir into the butter mixture.

3. Fold in the flour and the chopped blackberries, then divide the mixture between the two mugs and level the tops.

4. Transfer the mugs to a microwave and cook on full power for 1 ½ minutes until a skewer inserted into the centre comes out clean. If not, return to the microwave for 15 seconds and test again. Leave the cakes to cool completely.

5. To decorate, whip the cream with an electric whisk until it holds its shape. It should be of piping consistency.

6. Mix the icing sugar with the cream cheese until combined. Spread a layer of the sweetened cheese onto the tops of the cakes and smooth with a palette knife.

7. Spoon the cream into a piping bag fitted with a medium plain nozzle and pipe a generous pillow of fresh cream on top of the cheese layer.

8. Arrange the fresh blackberries in the centre and dust with icing sugar before serving.

97

Sour cream and raspberry

MAKES: 1 | PREP TIME: 15 MINUTES | COOKING TIME: 1 MINUTE

INGREDIENTS

30 ml / 1 oz / 2 tbsp sour cream

30 ml / 1 oz / 2 tbsp whole milk

½ tbsp sunflower oil

¼ lemon, juiced

50 g / 1 ¾ oz / ⅓ cup self-raising flour

2 tbsp caster (superfine) sugar

5 fresh raspberries

2 tbsp icing (confectioner's) sugar

METHOD

1. Mix half of the sour cream with the milk, and lemon juice in a small mug. Add the flour and caster sugar and stir well, then poke the raspberries into the mixture.

2. Transfer the mug to a microwave and cook on full power for 1 minute until a skewer comes out clean. If not, return to the microwave for 10 seconds and test again. Leave to cool for 5 minutes.

3. Mix the remaining sour cream with the icing sugar and drizzle it over the top before serving.

Lime and mint

MAKES: 2 | PREP TIME: 5 MINUTES | COOKING TIME: 1 MINUTE, 30 SECONDS

INGREDIENTS

55 g / 2 oz / ¼ cup butter, softened

55 g / 2 oz / ¼ cup caster (superfine) sugar

1 large egg, beaten

55 g / 2 oz / ⅓ cup self-raising flour

1 lime, juice and zest

a handful of mint leaves, finely chopped

½ tsp green food colouring

METHOD

1. In a mixing bowl, beat the butter and sugar together until pale and smooth. Add the egg and mix through.

2. Sift the flour into the bowl and fold through to form a batter, then fold through the rest of the ingredients.

3. Spoon the mixture into two mugs or microwaveable glasses and level off the tops.

4. Transfer the mugs to a microwave and cook on full power for 1 ½ minutes until a skewer inserted into the centre comes out clean. If not, return to the microwave for 15 seconds and test again.

5. Allow to cool. If desired, decorate with a sprinkle of dessicated coconut, lime zest and a mint leaf.

Chocolate orange

MAKES: 1 | PREP TIME: 5 MINUTES | COOKING TIME: 1 MINUTE, 30 SECONDS

INGREDIENTS

40 g / 1 ½ oz / ¼ cup self-raising flour

40 g / 1 ½ oz / ¼ cup caster (superfine) sugar

20 g / ¾ oz / ⅛ cup cocoa powder

1 medium egg

2 tbsp milk

2 tbsp vegetable oil

1 tbsp chocolate chips

zest of ½ small orange, reserving some as garnish

METHOD

1. Mix the flour, sugar and cocoa in a large mug. Add the egg and mix thoroughly.

2. Combine the milk and oil in another mug, then add to the batter and stir.

3. Fold in the chocolate chips and the orange zest.

4. Place the mug in the centre of the microwave and cook for 1 ½ minutes until a skewer inserted into the centre comes out clean. If not, return to the microwave for 15 seconds and test again.

5. Garnish with the remaining zest and serve.

Summer fruits

MAKES: 1 | PREP TIME: 5 MINUTES | COOKING TIME: 2 MINUTES

INGREDIENTS

30 g / 1 oz / ⅛ cup butter, softened

30 g / 1 oz / ⅛ cup caster (superfine) sugar

1 medium egg

30 g / 1 oz / ⅛ cup self-raising flour

1 tbsp milk

1 tbsp frozen mixed berries (defrosted)

FOR THE TOPPING

1 tbsp frozen mixed berries (defrosted)

1 tbsp strawberry jam (jelly)

METHOD

1. Mix the butter and sugar in a large mug. Add the egg and stir until well mixed.

2. Gradually stir in the flour, then add the milk and mix well before folding in the berries.

3. Place the mug in the centre of the microwave and cook for 1 ½ minutes until well risen or until a skewer inserted in the centre comes out clean. Allow to cool.

4. For the topping, combine the frozen berries and jam in a separate mug, then cook for 30 seconds.

5. Spoon the cooked berries onto the cake and serve.

Citrus zest

MAKES: 2 | PREP TIME: 10 MINUTES | COOKING TIME: 1 MINUTE, 30 SECONDS

INGREDIENTS

55 g / 2 oz / ¼ cup butter, softened

55 g / 2 oz / ¼ cup caster (superfine) sugar

1 large egg

1 tsp orange extract

55 g / 2 oz / ⅓ cup self-raising flour, sifted

½ lemon, zested

½ lime, zested

TO DECORATE

30 g / 1 oz / ½ cup butter, softened

75 g / 2 ½ oz / ¾ cup icing (confectioner's) sugar,
plus extra for dusting

1 tsp orange extract

1 tsp green sugar balls

METHOD

1. Beat the butter and sugar together in a mug until pale and smooth.

2. Break the egg into a second mug and add the orange extract. Beat gently, then gradually stir into the butter mixture.

3. Fold in the flour and stir through the lemon and lime zest, then divide the mixture between the two mugs and level the tops.

4. Transfer the mugs to a microwave and cook on full power for 1 ½ minutes until a skewer inserted into the centre comes out clean. If not, return to the microwave for 15 seconds and test again. Leave to cool completely.

5. To decorate, beat the butter, icing sugar and orange extract together until pale and creamy, adding a few drops of hot water if the mixture is too stiff.

6. Spoon the buttercream into a piping bag fitted with a medium plain nozzle and pipe a spiral swirl on top of each cake.

7. Decorate with the green sugar balls.

Very berry

MAKES: 2 | PREP TIME: 15 MINUTES | COOKING TIME: 1 MINUTE, 30 SECONDS

INGREDIENTS

55 g / 2 oz / ¼ cup butter, softened

55 g / 2 oz / ¼ cup caster (superfine) sugar

1 large egg

55 g / 2 oz / ⅓ cup self-raising flour, sifted

3 tbsp mixed berries, defrosted if frozen

TO DECORATE

30 g / 1 oz / ½ cup butter, softened

75 g / 2 ½ oz / ¾ cup icing (confectioner's) sugar

2 tbsp mixed berries, defrosted if frozen

METHOD

1. Beat the butter and sugar together in a mug until pale and smooth.

2. Break the egg into a second mug and beat gently with a fork, then gradually stir into the butter mixture.

3. Fold in the flour, followed by the berries, then divide the mixture between the two mugs and level the tops.

4. Transfer the mugs to a microwave and cook on full power for 1 ½ minutes until a skewer inserted into the centre comes out clean. If not, return to the microwave for 15 seconds and test again. Leave to cool completely.

5. To decorate, beat the butter and icing sugar together until pale and well whipped, adding a few drops of hot water if the mixture is too stiff.

6. Spoon the buttercream into a piping bag fitted with a large star nozzle and pipe a big ring on top of each cake. Fill the centre of the rings with berries and serve immediately.

Spiced apple

MAKES: 2 | PREP TIME: 15 MINUTES | COOKING TIME: 2 MINUTES

INGREDIENTS

1 apple, cored and chopped

1 tbsp butter

½ tsp cinnamon

½ tsp allspice

1 tbsp brown sugar

55 g / 2 oz / ¼ cup butter, softened

55 g / 2 oz / ¼ cup caster (superfine) sugar

1 large egg, beaten

55 g / 2 oz / ⅓ cup self-raising flour

METHOD

1. Place the apple, butter, cinnamon, allspice and brown sugar into a saucepan. Gently heat and stir to melt the sugar and until the apples start to break down a little. Remove from the heat and set some of the apple aside as a topping.

2. In a mixing bowl, beat the butter and sugar together until pale and creamy. Add the egg to the bowl and mix through.

3. Sift the flour into the bowl and fold through to form a batter.

4. Stir the apples from the saucepan into the batter before dividing between two large mugs.

5. Place the mugs into a microwave and cook on full power for 2 minutes until a skewer inserted into the centre comes out clean. If not, return to the microwave for 15 seconds and test again.

6. Serve the cakes with the reserved apple pieces on top as garnish.

Gluten-free banana sponge

MAKES: 1 | PREP TIME: 5 MINUTES | COOKING TIME: 1 MINUTE

INGREDIENTS

1 ripe banana

2 tbsp almond butter

1 tsp baking powder

1 egg, beaten

1 tbsp icing (confectioner's) sugar

2 tbsp water

sprinkles

METHOD

1. Place the banana into a mug and mash.

2. Add the almond butter, baking powder and egg, mixing to form a batter.

3. Place into the microwave and cook on full for 1 minute until risen and a skewer inserted into the cake comes out clean. Microwave for a further 15 seconds if not ready.

4. To decorate, mix together the icing sugar and water to make the icing.

5. Spoon the icing onto the cake and top with sprinkles.

Lemon fancy

MAKES: 2 | PREP TIME: 10 MINUTES | COOKING TIME: 2 MINUTES

INGREDIENTS

65 g / 2 oz / ¼ cup butter, softened

50 g / 1 ¾ oz / ¼ cup caster (superfine) sugar, plus 2 tbsp

1 large egg

2 tbsp whole milk

1 lemon, juiced and zest finely pared

55 g / 2 oz / ⅓ cup self-raising flour, sifted

½ tbsp cornflour (cornstarch)

2 sprigs mint

METHOD

1. Beat the butter and sugar together in a large mug until pale and smooth.

2. Break the egg into a second large mug and add the milk and half of the lemon zest. Beat gently, then stir into the butter mixture.

3. Fold in the flour, then divide the mixture between the two mugs and level the tops.

4. To decorate, mix the remaining lemon zest, 2 tablespoons of caster sugar and cornflour. Sprinkle it over the top of the cake mixture.

5. Stir 200 ml of boiling water into the lemon juice, then spoon it over the cakes.

6. Transfer the mugs to a microwave and cook on full power for 2 minutes or until well risen and springy on top.

7. Leave the cakes to cool for a few minutes before serving, garnished with mint.

Chocolate and blueberry

MAKES: 2 | PREP TIME: 15 MINUTES | COOKING TIME: 1 MINUTE, 30 SECONDS

INGREDIENTS

55 g / 2 oz / ¼ cup butter, softened
55 g / 2 oz / ¼ cup caster (superfine) sugar
1 large egg
55 g / 2 oz / ⅓ cup self-raising flour, sifted
2 tbsp unsweetened cocoa powder
2 tbsp blueberry jam (jelly)

TO DECORATE

30 g / 1 oz / ½ cup butter, softened
75 g / 2 ½ oz / ¾ cup icing (confectioner's) sugar
1 tbsp unsweetened cocoa powder

METHOD

1. Beat the butter and sugar together in a mug until pale and smooth.

2. Break the egg into a second mug. Beat gently, then gradually stir into the butter mixture. Fold in the flour and cocoa, then divide the mixture between the two mugs. Level the tops, then add a spoonful of blueberry jam to each one.

3. Transfer the mugs to a microwave and cook on full power for 1 ½ minutes. Leave to cool.

4. To decorate, beat the butter, icing sugar and most of the cocoa together until well whipped. Spoon the buttercream into a piping bag fitted with a large star nozzle and pipe a big swirl on top of each cake. Sprinkle with cocoa and fresh blueberries, if desired.

Orange and cranberry

MAKES: 1 | PREP TIME: 10 MINUTES | COOKING TIME: 1 MINUTE, 30 SECONDS

INGREDIENTS

30 g / 1 oz butter, softened

30 g / 1 oz caster (superfine) sugar

1 medium egg

30 g / 1 oz self-raising flour

1 tbsp milk

2 tbsp dried cranberries soaked
in 1 tsp orange liqueur

zest of ½ orange

1 tbsp orange juice

1 segment of satsuma

METHOD

1. Mix the butter and sugar in a large mug.
   Add the egg and stir until well mixed.

2. Gradually stir in the flour, then add the milk
   and mix well.

3. Fold in 1 tablespoon of the soaked
   cranberries, orange zest and juice.

4. Place the mug in the centre of the microwave
   and cook for 1 ½ minutes until well risen or
   until a skewer inserted in the centre comes
   out clean.

5. Top with more soaked cranberries and the
   satsuma segment.

111

Strawberry delight

MAKES: 2 | PREP TIME: 15 MINUTES | COOKING TIME: 3 MINUTES

INGREDIENTS

3 egg whites

¼ tsp cream of tartar

65 g / 2 ⅓ oz / ⅓ cup caster (superfine) sugar

50 g / 1 ¾ oz / ⅓ cup self-raising flour

a pinch of salt

strawberries for garnish

METHOD

1. Using an electric whisk, whisk the egg whites in a clean bowl until foamy. Add the cream of tartar and whisk for 1 minute.

2. Gradually add the sugar whilst whisking until fully mixed and stiff peaks form.

3. Sieve the self-raising flour and salt together. Using a spatula, gradually fold into the eggs until well mixed to form a smooth batter.

4. Divide the mixture between two large mugs. One at a time, place the mugs in the centre of the microwave and cook for 1 ½ minutes at 60% power, checking the cake at 30 second intervals until a skewer comes out clean.

5. Serve garnished with fresh strawberries.

112

Apple and cinnamon

MAKES: 2 | PREP TIME: 15 MINUTES | COOKING TIME: 1 MINUTE, 30 SECONDS

INGREDIENTS

55 g / 2 oz / ¼ cup butter, softened

55 g / 2 oz / ¼ cup caster (superfine) sugar

1 large egg

55 g / 2 oz / ⅓ cup self-raising flour, sifted

½ tsp ground cinnamon, plus extra for sprinkling

½ eating apple, peeled, cored and diced

150 ml / 5 ½ fl. oz / ⅔ cup double (heavy) cream

METHOD

1. Beat the butter and sugar together in a mug until pale and smooth.

2. Gently beat the egg in second mug, then gradually stir into the butter mixture.

3. Fold in the flour, cinnamon and apple, then divide the mixture between the two mugs.

4. Transfer the mugs to a microwave and cook on full power for 1 ½ minutes until a skewer inserted into the centre comes out clean. Leave to cool completely.

5. Whip the cream until stiffened, then spoon into a piping bag fitted with a large star nozzle. Pipe swirl on top of each cake and sprinkle with cinnamon.

Blueberry sponge

MAKES: 2 | PREP TIME: 10 MINUTES | COOKING TIME: 1 MINUTE, 30 SECONDS

INGREDIENTS

55 g / 2 oz / ¼ cup butter, softened

55 g / 2 oz / ¼ cup caster (superfine) sugar

1 large egg

1 tsp lemon zest, finely grated

55 g / 2 oz / ⅓ cup self-raising flour, sifted

1 handful of blueberries

icing (confectioner's) sugar, for dusting

METHOD

1. Beat the butter and sugar together in a mug until pale and smooth.

2. Gently beat the egg in a second mug and add the lemon zest, then stir into the butter mixture.

3. Fold in the flour, then divide the mixture between the two mugs. Push a few blueberries down into the centre of each and level the tops.

4. Transfer the mugs to a microwave and cook on full power for 1 ½ minutes until a skewer inserted into the centre comes out clean.

5. Leave the cakes to cool for 5 minutes. Dust lightly with icing sugar and garnish with the rest of the blueberries.

Apple and berry

MAKES: 1 | PREP TIME: 15 MINUTES | COOKING TIME: 1 MINUTE, 30 SECONDS

INGREDIENTS

30 g / 1 oz butter, softened

30 g / 1 oz caster (superfine) sugar

1 medium egg

30 g / 1 oz self-raising flour

1 tbsp milk

FOR THE COMPOTE

½ apple, finely cubed

2 large strawberries, diced

1 small handful of blackberries

1 tbsp caster (superfine) sugar

METHOD

1. For the compote, place the apple, strawberries and blackberries in a microwaveable bowl with the sugar and mix well.

2. Cook in the microwave for 2 minutes, stir and set aside to cool.

3. Mix the butter and sugar in a large mug. Add the egg and stir until well mixed. Gradually stir in the flour, then add the milk and mix well.

4. Stir in half of the apple and berry compote.

5. Place the mug in the centre of the microwave and cook for 1 ½ minutes until well risen or until a skewer inserted in the centre comes out clean.

6. Serve with a spoonful of the remaining compote.

115

Banana and cinnamon

MAKES: 2 | PREP TIME: 15 MINUTES | COOKING TIME: 1 MINUTE, 30 SECONDS

INGREDIENTS

55 g / 2 oz / ¼ cup butter, softened

55 g / 2 oz / ¼ cup caster (superfine) sugar

1 small banana, peeled

1 large egg

55 g / 2 oz / ⅓ cup self-raising flour, sifted

1 tsp ground cinnamon, plus extra for sprinkling

150 ml / 5 ½ fl. oz / ⅔ cup double (heavy) cream

METHOD

1. Beat the butter and sugar together in a mug until pale and smooth.

2. Mash the banana in a second mug, then break the egg and beat them gently together.

3. Gradually combine the two mixtures, then fold in the flour and cinnamon. Divide the mixtures between the two mugs and level the tops.

4. Transfer the mugs to a microwave and cook on full power for 1 ½ minutes or until risen and the tops spring back when prodded.

5. Whip the cream until stiff, then spoon it into a piping bag fitted with a large star nozzle. Pipe a swirl of cream on top and sprinkle with cinnamon.

Raspberry pavlova

MAKES: 2 | PREP TIME: 20 MINUTES | COOKING TIME: 1 MINUTE, 30 SECONDS

INGREDIENTS

55 g / 2 oz / ¼ cup butter, softened

55 g / 2 oz / ¼ cup caster (superfine) sugar

1 large egg

55 g / 2 oz / ⅓ cup self-raising flour, sifted

2 tbsp fresh raspberries, chopped

TO DECORATE

250 ml / 9 fl. oz / 1 cup fresh whipping cream

6 fresh raspberries

2 mini meringues (see Toppings chapter for recipe)

METHOD

1. Beat the butter and sugar together in a mug until pale and glossy.

2. Gently beat the egg in a second mug, then gradually stir into the butter mixture. Fold in rest of the ingredients, then divide between the two mugs and level the tops.

3. Put the mugs in a microwave and cook for 1 ½ minutes until a skewer inserted into the centre comes out clean. If not, return to the microwave for 15 seconds and test again.

4. Whip the cream with an electric whisk until it is light and fluffy and holds its shape. Spoon the cream into a piping bag fitted with a small plain nozzle and pipe teardrops around the outsides of the cakes. Arrange the fresh raspberries in the centre and top with a mini meringue before serving.

Cherry and berry

MAKES: 2 | PREP TIME: 15 MINUTES | COOKING TIME: 1 MINUTE, 30 SECONDS

INGREDIENTS

55 g / 2 oz / ¼ cup butter, softened

55 g / 2 oz / ¼ cup caster (superfine) sugar

1 large egg

55 g / 2 oz / ⅓ cup self-raising flour, sifted

3 tbsp chunky black cherry pie filling

TO DECORATE

30 g / 1 oz / ½ cup butter, softened

75 g / 2 ½ oz / ¾ cup icing (confectioner's) sugar

½ tsp vanilla extract

2 tbsp mixed berry jam (see Toppings chapter for recipe)

METHOD

1. Beat the butter and sugar together in a mug until pale and smooth.

2. Gently beat the egg in a second mug and then gradually stir into the butter mixture.

3. Fold in the flour and swirl in the cherry pie filling, then divide the mixture between the two mugs and level the tops.

4. Transfer the mugs to a microwave and cook on full power for 1 ½ minutes until a skewer inserted into the centre comes out clean. If not, return to the microwave for 15 seconds and test again. Leave the cakes to cool.

5. To decorate, beat the butter, icing sugar and vanilla extract together until pale and well whipped, adding a few drops of hot water if the mixture is too stiff.

6. Spoon the buttercream into a piping bag fitted with a small plain nozzle and pipe teardrops around one side of each cake.

7. Spoon the jam onto the tops and serve.

Mug Cakes

Indulgent mug cakes

Chocolate mousse

MAKES: 1 | PREP TIME: 5 MINUTES | COOKING TIME: 1 MINUTE, 30 SECONDS

INGREDIENTS

80 g / 2 ¾ oz dark chocolate

1 tbsp butter

1 tbsp sugar

1 egg, separated

METHOD

1. Finely chop the chocolate and place into a mug with the butter. Heat in a microwave for 10 seconds at a time until melted. Stir to mix and set aside to cool.

2. Add a pinch of the sugar to the egg yolk and beat until thick and creamy.

3. Add the remaining sugar to the egg whites and whisk until soft peaks appear.

4. Beat the egg yolks into the melted chocolate before folding into the egg whites, taking care not to beat the air out of the mixture. It may be easier to do this in the bowl with the egg white rather than in the mug.

5. Return the mixture to the mug and cook on full power for 1 ½ minute before removing and checking. The surface of the cake should be slightly firm but it will still be runny underneath. Microwave for a further 15 seconds at a time if not cooked enough.

Cookies and cream

MAKES: 2 | PREP TIME: 15 MINUTES | COOKING TIME: 1 MINUTE, 30 SECONDS

INGREDIENTS

55 g / 2 oz / ¼ cup butter, softened

55 g / 2 oz / ¼ cup caster (superfine) sugar

1 large egg

55 g / 2 oz / ⅓ cup self-raising flour, sifted

4 mini chocolate cookies, roughly chopped

TO DECORATE

30 g / 1 oz / ½ cup butter, softened

75 g / 2 ½ oz / ¾ cup icing (confectioner's) sugar, plus extra for dusting

½ tsp vanilla extract

4 mini chocolate cookies

METHOD

1. Beat the butter and sugar together in a mug until pale and smooth.

2. Gently beat the egg in a second mug, then gradually stir into the butter mixture.

3. Fold in the flour and chopped cookies, then divide the mixture between the two mugs and level the tops.

4. Transfer the mugs to a microwave and cook on full power for 1 ½ minutes until a skewer inserted into the centre comes out clean. If not, return to the microwave for 15 seconds and test again. Leave to cool completely.

5. To decorate, beat the butter, icing sugar and vanilla extract together until pale and well whipped, adding a few drops of hot water if the mixture is too stiff.

6. Spoon the buttercream into a piping bag and pipe a big swirl on top of each cake.

7. Crumble two of the cookies into crumbs and sprinkle on top before garnishing each cake with a whole cookie.

Banoffee treat

MAKES: 1 | PREP TIME: 5 MINUTES | COOKING TIME: 1 MINUTE, 30 SECONDS

INGREDIENTS

30 g / 1 oz / ⅛ cup butter, softened

30 g / 1 oz / ⅛ cup caster (superfine) sugar

1 medium egg, beaten

30 g / 1 oz / ⅛ cup self-raising flour

1 tbsp milk

½ banana, mashed

TO DECORATE

½ banana, sliced

2 tbsp toffee sauce

METHOD

1. In a large mug, mix the butter and sugar until smooth. Gently add the egg, stirring well to combine.

2. Gradually stir in the flour, then add the milk and mix well before stirring in the mashed banana.

3. Place the mug in the centre of the microwave and cook for 1 ½ minutes until well risen or until a skewer inserted in the centre comes out clean.

4. Decorate with slices of banana and drizzle with toffee sauce.

Malted chocolate

MAKES: 2 | PREP TIME: 30 MINUTES | COOKING TIME: 16 MINUTES

INGREDIENTS

55 g / 2 oz / ¼ cup butter, softened

55 g / 2 oz / ¼ cup caster (superfine) sugar

1 large egg

55 g / 2 oz / ⅓ cup self-raising flour, sifted

1 tbsp cocoa powder

TO DECORATE

4 tbsp chocolate spread

1 small packet of malted chocolate balls

1 tbsp cocoa powder, plus extra for dusting

METHOD

1. Preheat the oven to 160°C (140°C fan) / 350F / gas 4.

2. Beat the butter and sugar together in an ovenproof mug until pale and smooth.

3. Gently beat the egg in a second ovenproof mug, then gradually stir into the butter mixture.

4. Fold in the flour and cocoa powder and mix well to combine. Divide the mixture between the two mugs and level the tops.

5. Transfer to a baking tray and cook in the centre of the oven for 16 minutes until a skewer inserted into the centre comes out clean.

6. To serve, spread the tops of the cakes with the chocolate spread. Cover with malted chocolate balls and dust with cocoa powder.

Red velvet

MAKES: 1 | PREP TIME: 10 MINUTES | COOKING TIME: 1 MINUTE, 30 SECONDS

INGREDIENTS

30 g / 1 oz butter, softened

30 g / 1 oz caster (superfine) sugar

1 medium egg, beaten

1 tbsp milk

1 tbsp red food dye

30 g / 1 oz self-raising flour

20 g cocoa powder

FOR THE FROSTING

20 g cream cheese

20 g icing (confectioner's) sugar

red sugar sprinkles

METHOD

1. Mix the butter and sugar in a large mug. Add the egg and stir.

2. In a separate mug, combine the milk and food dye.

3. Gradually incorporate the flour and cocoa powder into the butter mixture, then add the milk and mix well.

4. Place the mug in the centre of the microwave and cook for 1 ½ minutes or until a skewer inserted in the centre comes out clean.

5. To make the frosting, combine the cream cheese and icing sugar. Top the cooled cake with the frosting and sugar sprinkles.

130

Black Forest

MAKES: 1 | PREP TIME: 5 MINUTES | COOKING TIME: 1 MINUTE, 30 SECONDS

INGREDIENTS

75 g / 3 oz / ½ cup self-raising flour

75 g / 3 oz / ½ cup caster (superfine) sugar

50 g / 2 oz / ¼ cup cocoa powder

1 large egg, beaten

50 ml / 2 fl. oz / ¼ cup milk

50 ml / 2 oz / ¼ cup vegetable oil

2 tbsp chocolate chips

2 tbsp canned pitted black cherries

2 tbsp kirsch or cherry liqueur

METHOD

1. Mix the flour, sugar and cocoa powder in a large mug. Add the egg and mix thoroughly.

2. In a separate mug, combine the milk and oil, then add to the batter and stir.

3. Fold in the chocolate chips, cherries and liqueur. Divide the mixture between the two mugs and level the tops.

4. Place the mugs in the centre of the microwave and cook for 1 ½ minutes on full power or until a skewer inserted into the centre comes out clean.

5. Allow to cool a little, then serve garnished with an additional cherry if desired.

131

Marshmallow heart

MAKES: 2 | PREP TIME: 10 MINUTES | COOKING TIME: 1 MINUTE, 30 SECONDS

INGREDIENTS

55 g / 2 oz / ¼ cup butter, softened

55 g / 2 oz / ¼ cup caster (superfine) sugar

1 large egg, beaten

55 g / 2 oz / ⅓ cup self-raising flour

1 tbsp cocoa

2 pink marshmallows

icing (confectioner's) sugar to dust

METHOD

1. In a mixing bowl, beat the butter and sugar together until pale and smooth. Add the egg and mix through. Sift the flour and cocoa into the bowl and fold through to form a batter.

2. Divide the mixture between two mugs and level the tops.

3. Transfer to a microwave and cook on full power for 1 ½ minutes or until a skewer inserted in the centre comes out clean.

4. Use a heart shaped cookie cutter to create a hole, then insert the marshmallow. Allow to cool before serving with a dusting of icing sugar.

Melt-in-the-middle caramel

MAKES: 2 | PREP TIME: 20 MINUTES | COOKING TIME: 1 MINUTE, 30 SECONDS

INGREDIENTS

55 g / 2 oz / ¼ cup butter, softened

55 g / 2 oz / ¼ cup caster (superfine) sugar

1 large egg

55 g / 2 oz / ⅓ cup self-raising flour, sifted

1 ½ tbsp cocoa powder

6 squares caramel chocolate bar

METHOD

1. Beat the butter and sugar together in a mug until pale and smooth.

2. Gently beat the egg into a second mug, then gradually stir into the butter mixture.

3. Fold in the flour and cocoa powder, then divide the mixture between the two mugs. Press 3 squares of the chocolate down into the centre of each cake and level the tops.

4. Transfer the mugs to a microwave and cook on full power for 1 ½ minutes or until well risen. Leave to cool for 5 minutes before serving.

White chocolate and raspberry

MAKES: 1 | PREP TIME: 5 MINUTES | COOKING TIME: 2 MINUTES

INGREDIENTS

30 g / 1 oz butter, softened
30 g / 1 oz caster (superfine) sugar
1 medium egg, beaten
30 g / 1 oz self-raising flour
1 tbsp milk
1 tbsp white chocolate chips
1 tbsp freeze-dried raspberry pieces

TO DECORATE

1 tbsp white chocolate
fresh raspberries

METHOD

1. Mix the butter and sugar in a large mug. Add the egg and stir until well mixed.

2. Gradually stir in the flour, then add the milk and mix well. Fold in the chocolate chips with the freeze-dried raspberry pieces.

3. Place the mug in the centre of the microwave and cook for 1 ½ minutes until well risen or until a skewer inserted in the centre comes out clean.

4. Melt the white chocolate for 20 seconds in the microwave. Decorate with fresh raspberries and a drizzle of melted white chocolate.

Valentine's treat

MAKES: 2 | PREP TIME: 15 MINUTES | COOKING TIME: 1 MINUTE, 30 SECONDS

INGREDIENTS

55 g / 2 oz / ¼ cup butter, softened

55 g / 2 oz / ¼ cup caster (superfine) sugar

1 large egg

2 tsp red food colouring

55 g / 2 oz / ⅓ cup self-raising flour, sifted

1 tbsp unsweetened cocoa powder

½ tsp ground cinnamon

1 tbsp heart-shaped sugar confetti

METHOD

1. Beat the butter and sugar together in a mug until pale and smooth.

2. Gently beat the egg in a second mug with the food colouring, then gradually stir into the butter mixture.

3. Fold in the flour, cocoa and cinnamon. Divide the mixture between the two mugs and level the tops.

4. Transfer the mugs to a microwave and cook on full power for 1 ½ minutes until a skewer inserted in the centre comes out clean. If not, return to the microwave for 15 seconds and test again.

5. Leave to cool for 5 minutes, then garnish with sugar confetti.

Blue lava

MAKES: 2 | PREP TIME: 20 MINUTES | COOKING TIME: 2 MINUTES

INGREDIENTS

55 g / 2 oz / ¼ cup butter, softened

55 g / 2 oz / ¼ cup caster (superfine) sugar

1 large egg

55 g / 2 oz / ⅓ cup self-raising flour, sifted

2 tbsp unsweetened cocoa powder, plus extra
for sprinkling

30 g / 1 oz / ⅓ cup dark chocolate (minimum 60%
cocoa solids), broken into chunks

2 tbsp icing (confectioner's) sugar

a few drops blue food colouring

1 tbsp multi-coloured sugar strands

METHOD

1. Beat the butter and sugar together in a mug
   until pale and smooth.

2. Gently beat the egg in a second mug, then
   gradually stir into the butter mixture.

3. Fold in the flour and cocoa powder, then
   divide the mixture between the two mugs
   and level the tops. Arrange the chocolate
   chunks in the centre of each cake, then
   spoon half a tablespoon of water on top of
   each one.

4. Transfer the mugs to a microwave and cook
   on full power for 2 minutes.

5. Mix the icing sugar with just enough water
   to make a spoonable icing and colour it blue.

6. Use a small round cutter to remove a section
   from the top of each cake, revealing the
   molten centre below. Drizzle the icing over
   the cakes and decorate with sugar strands.

7. If desired, place some flavoured
   marshmallows in the centre to melt into
   the cake (see Toppings chapter for
   marshmallow recipe).

Hot chocolate

MAKES: 1 | PREP TIME: 5 MINUTES | COOKING TIME: 2 MINUTES

INGREDIENTS

30 g / 1 oz / ¼ cup plain (all-purpose) flour

1 tbsp cocoa

2 tsp caster (superfine) sugar

½ tsp baking powder

½ tsp cinnamon

50 ml / 1 ¾ fl. oz / ¼ cup milk

½ tbsp vegetable oil

a handful of mini marshmallows

2 tbsp chocolate chips

METHOD

1. Mix the flour, cocoa, sugar, baking powder and cinnamon in a mug.

2. Add the milk and oil and whisk together to form a batter. Drop a couple of marshmallows into the batter, reserving the rest for the topping.

3. Place into a microwave and cook on full power for 2 minutes until risen and the top of the cake is firm. Top with a tablespoon of chocolate chips and microwave again for 20 seconds or until evenly melted.

4. Top the cake with the remaining marshmallows and chocolate chips.

Vanilla fudge

MAKES: 1 | PREP TIME: 5 MINUTES | COOKING TIME: 1 MINUTE, 30 SECONDS

INGREDIENTS

30 g / 1 oz / ⅛ cup butter, softened

30 g / 1 oz / ⅛ cup caster (superfine) sugar

1 medium egg

30 g / 1 oz / ⅛ cup self-raising flour

1 tbsp milk

1 tsp vanilla extract

2 tbsp fudge pieces
(see Toppings chapter for recipe)

METHOD

1. Mix the butter and sugar in a large mug. Add the egg and stir until well mixed.

2. Gradually stir in the flour and add the milk and vanilla extract, mixing well, then fold in the fudge pieces.

3. Place the mug in the centre of the microwave and cook for 1 ½ minutes until well risen or until a skewer inserted in the centre comes out clean.

4. Allow to cool for a few minutes before serving.

139

Spiced chai

MAKES: 1 | PREP TIME: 5 MINUTES | COOKING TIME: 2 MINUTES

INGREDIENTS

1 egg

2 tbsp caster (superfine) sugar

1 tsp honey

2 tbsp butter, melted

½ tsp baking powder

50 g / 1 ¾ oz / ½ cup ground almonds

½ tsp ground allspice

¼ tsp ground ginger

¼ tsp ground star anise

½ tsp vanilla extract

2 tbsp whipped cream

1 tsp maple syrup

METHOD

1. Place the egg into a mug and mix in the sugar and honey until thick and glossy.

2. Add the butter, baking powder, almonds, allspice, ginger, star anise and vanilla extract and mix thoroughly until smooth.

3. Transfer to a microwave and cook on full power for 2 minutes until risen and the top of the cake is firm.

4. Remove for the microwave and serve with whipped cream and a drizzle of maple syrup.

Pistachio sponge

MAKES: 1 | PREP TIME: 5 MINUTES | COOKING TIME: 1 MINUTE, 30 SECONDS

INGREDIENTS

30 g / 1 oz butter, softened

30 g / 1 oz caster (superfine) sugar

1 tsp green food dye

1 medium egg

20 g self-raising flour

2 tbsp ground pistachios

1 tbsp milk

TO DECORATE

icing (confectioner's) sugar to sprinkle

1 whole pistachio nut

METHOD

1. Mix the butter, sugar and food dye in a large mug.

2. Add the egg and stir until well mixed.

3. Gradually stir in the flour and ground pistachios. Add the milk, then mix well.

4. Place the mug in the centre of the microwave and cook for 1 ½ minutes until well risen or until a skewer inserted in the centre comes out clean.

5. Dust with icing sugar and top with the whole pistachio nut.

Rocky road

MAKES: 2 | PREP TIME: 15 MINUTES | COOKING TIME: 1 MINUTE, 30 SECONDS

INGREDIENTS

55 g / 2 oz / ¼ cup butter, softened

55 g / 2 oz / ¼ cup caster (superfine) sugar

1 large egg

55 g / 2 oz / ⅓ cup self-raising flour, sifted

1 tbsp cocoa powder

1 tbsp dried cranberries

1 tbsp milk chocolate chunks

1 tbsp chopped mixed nuts

TO DECORATE

30 g / 1 oz / ½ cup butter, softened

75 g / 2 ½ oz / ¾ cup icing (confectioner's) sugar, plus extra for dusting

1 tbsp cocoa powder

6 tbsp milk chocolate chunks

8 marshmallows

METHOD

1. Beat the butter and sugar together in a mug until pale and smooth.

2. Gently beat the egg in a second mug, then gradually stir into the butter mixture.

3. Fold in the flour and cocoa powder, followed by the cranberries, chocolate chunks and nuts. Divide the mixture between the two mugs and level the tops.

4. Transfer the mugs to a microwave and cook on full power for 1 ½ minutes until a skewer inserted in the centre comes out clean. If not, return to the microwave for 15 seconds and test again. Leave the cakes to cool completely.

5. To decorate, beat the butter, icing sugar and cocoa together until pale and well whipped, adding a few drops of hot water if the mixture is too stiff.

6. Spoon the buttercream onto the cakes and top with 2 tablespoons of the chocolate chunks and the marshmallows.

7. Put the rest of the chocolate chunks in a mug. Melt in the microwave on medium in 5 second bursts until melted, stirring in between.

8. Drizzle over the cakes and dust with icing sugar.

Stout pudding

MAKES: 2 | PREP TIME: 10 MINUTES | COOKING TIME: 2 MINUTES

INGREDIENTS

150 ml / 5 ¼ fl. oz / ⅔ cup stout

50 g / 1 ¾ oz / ½ cup sugar

1 tbsp butter

75 g / 2 ½ oz / ½ cup plain (all-purpose) flour

1 tsp baking powder

1 tbsp cocoa powder

1 egg, beaten

METHOD

1. Place the stout, sugar and butter into a clean microwavable bowl. Microwave on full for 30 seconds to melt the butter and whisk to dissolve the sugar.

2. Combine the flour, baking powder and cocoa in a mixing bowl. Add the stout mixture and whisk together, adding the egg once the batter has formed.

3. Divide between two beer mugs and level off the surface.

4. Transfer to the microwave and cook on full power for 1 ½ minutes until a skewer inserted in the centre comes out clean. If not, microwave for a further 15 seconds.

5. Remove to cool for a couple of minutes before serving.

Chocolate and almond

MAKES: 2 | PREP TIME: 15 MINUTES | COOKING TIME: 1 MINUTE, 30 SECONDS

INGREDIENTS

55 g / 2 oz / ¼ cup butter, softened

55 g / 2 oz / ¼ cup light muscovado sugar

1 large egg

½ tsp almond extract

55 g / 2 oz / ⅓ cup self-raising flour, sifted

2 tbsp unsweetened cocoa powder

1 tbsp ground almonds

icing (confectioner's) sugar, for dusting

150 ml / 5 ½ fl. oz / ⅔ cup double (heavy) cream

1 tbsp almonds, chopped

METHOD

1. Beat the butter and sugar together in a mug until pale and smooth.

2. Gently beat the egg in a second mug with the almond extract, then gradually stir into the butter mixture.

3. Fold in the flour, cocoa and ground almonds, then divide the mixture between the two mugs and level the tops.

4. Transfer to a microwave and cook on full power for 1 ½ minutes or until well risen and the tops spring back when prodded. Leave to cool, then dust with icing sugar.

5. Whip the cream until it holds its shape, then spoon it onto the cakes and sprinkle with chopped almonds.

Sticky toffee

MAKES: 4 | PREP TIME: 15 MINUTES | COOKING TIME: 8-10 MINUTES

INGREDIENTS

90 g / 3 ¼ oz / ½ cup finely chopped, pitted dates, plus 4 whole dates to serve

90 ml / 3 fl. oz / ⅓ cup boiling water

40 g / 1 ½ oz / ¼ cup butter, softened

75 g / 2 ½ oz / ½ cup dark brown sugar

1 medium egg

90 g / 3 ¼ oz / ½ cup self-raising flour

½ tsp bicarbonate of (baking) soda

FOR THE TOFFEE SAUCE

2 tbsp dark brown sugar

2 tsp boiling water

1 tbsp double (heavy) cream

METHOD

1. Soak the finely-chopped dates in the boiling water for 5 minutes, then cook in the microwave for 2 minutes. Liquidize or mash and set aside.

2. In a bowl, mix the butter and the sugar and whisk until light and fluffy. Add the egg and whisk further.

3. Add the flour and bicarbonate of soda. Gently fold in the date mixture, then divide between the 4 mugs.

4. Place each mug in the centre of the microwave and cook for 1 ½ minutes or until a skewer inserted in the centre comes out clean.

5. To make the toffee sauce, stir the sugar and water in another mug and cook for 3 minutes. Stir in the cream and pour over the cakes.

147

Toffee waffle cream

MAKES: 2 | PREP TIME: 15 MINUTES | COOKING TIME: 1 MINUTE, 30 SECONDS

INGREDIENTS

55 g / 2 oz / ¼ cup butter, softened

55 g / 2 oz / ¼ cup light muscovado sugar

1 large egg

55 g / 2 oz / ⅓ cup self-raising flour, sifted

1 tsp ground cinnamon

150 ml / 5 ½ fl. oz / ⅔ cup double (heavy) cream

1 tbsp chocolate sauce

1 tbsp caramel sauce

1 toffee waffle, diced

METHOD

1. Beat the butter and sugar together in a mug until pale and smooth.

2. Gently beat the egg into a second mug, then gradually stir into the butter mixture.

3. Fold in the flour and cinnamon, then divide the mixture between the two mugs and level the tops.

4. Transfer the mugs to a microwave and cook on full power for 1 ½ minutes or until well risen and the tops spring back when prodded. Leave to cool.

5. Whip the cream until it holds its shape, then spoon it into a piping bag fitted with a large star nozzle. Pipe a big swirl of cream on top of each cake.

6. Drizzle with the sauces and scatter over the waffle pieces.

Chocolate lava

MAKES: 2 | PREP TIME: 10 MINUTES | COOKING TIME: 2 MINUTES

INGREDIENTS

55 g / 2 oz / ¼ cup butter, softened

55 g / 2 oz / ¼ cup caster (superfine) sugar

1 large egg

55 g / 2 oz / ⅓ cup self-raising flour, sifted

2 tbsp unsweetened cocoa powder,
plus extra for sprinkling

4 chocolate truffles

2 tbsp whipped cream

2 tbsp dark hot chocolate sauce

4 raspberries

METHOD

1. Beat the butter and sugar together in a mug
   until pale and smooth.

2. Gently beat the egg into a second mug, then
   gradually stir into the butter mixture.

3. Fold in the flour and cocoa powder, then divide
   the mixture between the two mugs and level
   the tops. Push two truffles into the centre of
   each cake, then spoon 1 tablespoon of water on
   top of each one.

4. Transfer the mugs to a microwave and cook on
   full power for 2 minutes.

5. Leave to cool for 5 minutes, then pipe a rosette
   of cream on top of each one. Drizzle with
   chocolate sauce and garnish with raspberries.

149

Salted caramel

MAKES: 1 | PREP TIME: 5 MINUTES | COOKING TIME: 5 MINUTES

INGREDIENTS

30 g / 1 oz / ⅛ cup butter

30 g / 1 oz / ⅛ cup caster (superfine) sugar

1 tsp vanilla extract

1 medium egg, beaten

30 g / 1 oz / ⅛ cup self-raising flour

1 tbsp milk

FOR THE CARAMEL SAUCE

2 tbsp caster (superfine) sugar

1 tbsp boiling water

2 tsp salted butter

1 tbsp double (heavy) cream

a pinch of salt

METHOD

1. Mix the butter, sugar and vanilla extract in a large mug. Add the egg and stir until well mixed, then gradually stir in the flour. Add the milk and mix well.

2. Place the mug in the centre of the microwave and cook for 1 ½ minutes until well risen or until a skewer inserted in the centre comes out clean.

3. For the caramel, combine the sugar and water in a clean mug. Cook in the microwave for up to 3 minutes or until the sugar has started to caramelize and turn golden brown.

4. Immediately add the butter, cream and salt. Stir carefully but quickly to combine.

5. Pour over the sponge and serve.

Caffè latte

MAKES: 1 | PREP TIME: 15 MINUTES | COOKING TIME: 1 MINUTE, 30 SECONDS

INGREDIENTS

55 g / 2 oz / ¼ cup butter, softened

55 g / 2 oz / ¼ cup caster (superfine) sugar

1 large egg, beaten

2 tbsp sweetened coffee and chicory essence

55 g / 2 oz / ⅓ cup self-raising flour, sifted

TO DECORATE

30 g / 1 oz / ½ cup butter, softened

½ tsp vanilla extract

75 g / 2 ½ oz / ¾ cup icing (confectioner's) sugar

2 chocolate-covered coffee beans

METHOD

1. Beat the butter and sugar together in a mug until pale and silky, then gradually stir the egg and coffee essence into the mixture. Fold in the flour and combine well.

2. Divide the mixture between two mugs and level the tops. Transfer to a microwave and cook on full power for 1 ½ minutes until a skewer inserted into the centre comes out clean. If not, return to the microwave for 15 seconds and test again. Leave to cool.

3. Make the decoration by beating the butter, vanilla extract and icing sugar until pale and well whipped, adding a few drops of hot water if the mixture is too stiff. Put into a piping bag with a small plain nozzle and pipe teardrops onto the tops of each cake. Top with a chocolate-covered coffee bean.

151

Chai latte

MAKES: 2 | PREP TIME: 15 MINUTES | COOKING TIME: 1 MINUTE, 30 SECONDS

INGREDIENTS

55 g / 2 oz / ¼ cup butter, softened

55 g / 2 oz / ¼ cup light muscovado sugar

1 large egg

55 g / 2 oz / ⅓ cup self-raising flour, sifted

2 tsp chai latte powder

icing (confectioner's) sugar, for dusting

METHOD

1. Beat the butter and sugar together in a mug until pale and smooth.

2. Gently beat the egg in a second mug, then gradually stir into the butter mixture.

3. Fold in the flour and chai powder, then divide the mixture between the two mugs and level the tops.

4. Transfer the mugs to a microwave and cook on full power 1 ½ minutes until a skewer inserted into the centre comes out clean. If not, return to the microwave for 15 seconds and test again.

5. Leave the cakes to cool for 5 minutes before serving with a heavy dusting of icing sugar.

Spiced chocolate

MAKES: 2 | PREP TIME: 5 MINUTES | COOKING TIME: 4 MINUTES

INGREDIENTS

50 g / 1 ¾ oz / ½ cup self-raising flour

2 tbsp cocoa powder, plus extra to dust

1 tsp cinnamon

50 g / 1 ¾ oz / ½ cup caster (superfine) sugar

1 egg, beaten

50 ml / 1 ¾ fl. oz / ¼ cup milk

2 tbsp sunflower oil

1 tsp orange essence

1 tbsp hazelnut spread

a handful of mini marshmallows

METHOD

1. Combine the flour, cocoa, cinnamon and sugar in a mixing bowl, then beat in the egg.

2. Add the milk and oil and whisk to form a batter. Mix in the orange essence and hazelnut spread.

3. Divide the batter between two mugs and transfer to a microwave. Cook on full power for 4 minutes until risen and firm to the touch. Remove and set aside to cool.

4. Top with the marshmallows and dust the top of the cakes with additional cocoa powder.

153

Peanut butter and jam

MAKES: 2 | PREP TIME: 30 MINUTES | COOKING TIME: 1 MINUTE, 30 SECONDS

INGREDIENTS

55 g / 2 oz / ¼ cup butter, softened

55 g / 2 oz / ¼ cup caster (superfine) sugar

1 large egg, beaten

55 g / 2 oz / ⅓ cup self-raising flour, sifted

1 tbsp peanut butter

1 tbsp strawberry jam (jelly)

TO DECORATE

30 g / 1 oz / ½ cup butter, softened

75 g / 2 ½ oz / ¾ cup icing (confectioner's) sugar,
plus extra for dusting

2 tbsp peanut butter

1 tbsp strawberry jam (jelly)

METHOD

1. Beat the butter and sugar together in a mug
   until pale and smooth. Stir the beaten egg
   into the mixture, then fold in the flour,
   followed by the peanut butter and jam.

   Divide the mixture between two mugs and
   level the tops. Transfer to a microwave and
   cook on full power for 1 ½ minutes until a
   skewer inserted into the centre comes out
   clean. If not, return to the microwave for
   15 seconds and test again.

2. To decorate, beat the butter, icing sugar and
   peanut butter together until pale and well
   whipped. Spoon into a piping bag fitted with
   a large star nozzle and pipe a double ring
   round the edge of each cake. Fill the centre
   of each ring with strawberry jam.

Cinnamon cream

MAKES: 1 | PREP TIME: 8 MINUTES | COOKING TIME: 1 MINUTE, 30 SECONDS

INGREDIENTS

30 g / 1 oz / ⅛ cup butter, softened

30 g / 1 oz / ⅛ cup caster (superfine) sugar

1 tsp ground cinnamon

1 medium egg, beaten

30 g self-raising flour

1 tbsp milk

FOR THE TOPPING

1 tbsp caster (superfine) sugar

1 tsp boiling water

½ tsp ground cinnamon

20 g / ¾ oz / ¼ cup icing (confectioner's) sugar

10 g / ⅓ oz / ⅛ cup soft butter

METHOD

1. Mix the butter, sugar and cinnamon in a mug. Then stir in the egg, flour and milk.

2. Place the mug in the microwave and cook for 1 ½ minutes until risen and a skewer inserted into the centre comes out clean. Set aside.

3. In another mug, make the syrup by combining the caster sugar, water and cinnamon. Cook in the microwave for 2 minutes and then allow to cool.

4. To make the frosting, combine the icing sugar and butter to make the buttercream. Pipe onto the cake and then drizzle over the cinnamon syrup.

Rich chocolate chip

MAKES: 2 | PREP TIME: 15 MINUTES | COOKING TIME: 1 MINUTE, 30 SECONDS

INGREDIENTS

55 g / 2 oz / ¼ cup butter, softened

55 g / 2 oz / ¼ cup caster (superfine) sugar

1 large egg, beaten

55 g / 2 oz / ⅓ cup self-raising flour, sifted

1 tbsp cocoa powder

3 tbsp milk chocolate chunks

2 tbsp milk chocolate, melted

1 handful of white and dark chocolate chips

METHOD

1. Beat the butter and sugar together in a mug until pale and smooth, then gradually stir the egg into the butter mixture.

2. Fold in the flour, cocoa, and chocolate chunks, then divide the mixture between two mugs and level the tops.

3. Transfer to a microwave and cook for 1 ½ minutes until a skewer inserted into the centre comes out clean. Leave the cakes to stand for 5 minutes.

4. Pour 1 tablespoon of melted chocolate over each one. Sprinkle each mug cake with the chocolate chips and serve immediately.

Chocolate espresso

MAKES: 2 | PREP TIME: 10 MINUTES | COOKING TIME: 1 MINUTE, 30 SECONDS

INGREDIENTS

55 g / 2 oz / ¼ cup butter, softened

55 g / 2 oz / ¼ cup caster (superfine) sugar

1 large egg, beaten

55 g / 2 oz / ⅓ cup self-raising flour, sifted

1 tsp instant espresso powder

1 tbsp cocoa powder

TO DECORATE

30 g / 1 oz / ½ cup butter, softened

75 g / 2 ½ oz / ¾ cup icing (confectioner's) sugar

½ tsp instant espresso powder

METHOD

1. Beat the butter and sugar together in a mug until pale and smooth. Gradually stir the egg into the butter mixture, then fold in the flour, espresso powder and cocoa powder.

2. Divide the mixture between two mugs, level off the tops and transfer them to a microwave.

3. Cook on full power for 1 ½ minutes until a skewer inserted into the centre comes out clean. If not, return to the microwave for 15 seconds and test again. Leave the cakes to cool completely.

4. To decorate, beat the butter, icing sugar and espresso powder together until pale and well whipped, adding a few drops of hot water if the mixture is too stiff. Spoon or pipe onto the cakes and dust with cocoa powder.

Mocha sponge

MAKES: 2 | PREP TIME: 15 MINUTES | COOKING TIME: 1 MINUTE, 30 SECONDS

INGREDIENTS

55 g / 2 oz / ¼ cup butter, softened

55 g / 2 oz / ¼ cup caster (superfine) sugar

1 large egg, beaten

55 g / 2 oz / ⅓ cup self-raising flour

1 tbsp cocoa

50 g / 1 ¾ oz / ½ cup dark chocolate, finely chopped

1 espresso coffee, cooled

METHOD

1. In a mixing bowl, beat the butter and sugar together until pale and smooth. Add the egg to the bowl and mix through the butter and sugar.

2. Sift the flour and cocoa into the bowl and fold through to form a batter. Fold half the chocolate and the coffee into the batter.

3. Spoon the mixture into two mugs and smooth off the tops.

4. Transfer the mugs to a microwave and cook on full power for 1 ½ minutes until a skewer inserted into the centre comes out clean. If not, return to the microwave for 15 seconds and test again.

5. Remove to cool for a couple of minutes before topping with the rest of the chopped chocolate.

Chocolate and star anise

MAKES: 2 | PREP TIME: 15 MINUTES | COOKING TIME: 1 MINUTE, 30 SECONDS

INGREDIENTS

55 g / 2 oz / ¼ cup butter, softened

55 g / 2 oz / ¼ cup caster (superfine) sugar

1 large egg, beaten

55 g / 2 oz / ⅓ cup self-raising flour, sifted

2 tbsp unsweetened cocoa powder

½ tsp ground star anise, plus extra for sprinkling

2 tbsp dark hot chocolate sauce
(see Toppings chapter)

METHOD

1. Beat the butter and sugar together in a mug until pale and smooth, then gradually stir in the egg.

2. Fold in the flour, cocoa and star anise, then divide the mixture between two mugs and level the tops.

3. Transfer the mugs to a microwave and cook on full power for 1 ½ minutes or until well risen and springy.

4. Leave the cakes to cool for 5 minutes, then top with chocolate sauce and add an extra sprinkle of ground star anise.

Christmas chocolate

MAKES: 2 | PREP TIME: 5 MINUTES | COOKING TIME: 4 MINUTES

INGREDIENTS

50 g / 1 ¾ oz / ½ cup self-raising flour
2 tbsp cocoa powder, plus extra to dust
½ tsp cinnamon
½ tsp nutmeg
½ tsp ginger
50 g / 1 ¾ oz / ½ cup caster (superfine) sugar
1 egg, beaten
50 ml / 1 ¾ fl. oz / ¼ cup milk
2 tbsp sunflower oil
1 clementine, zest only
2 tbsp mini marshmallows

METHOD

1. Combine the flour, cocoa, spices and sugar in a mixing bowl, then beat in the egg.

2. Add the milk and oil and whisk to form a batter. Mix in the clementine zest.

3. Divide the batter between two mugs and place the mini marshmallows on top.

4. Transfer to a microwave and cook on full power for 4 minutes until risen and firm to the touch. Remove and set aside to cool.

5. Dust the top of the cakes with additional cocoa powder to cover the marshmallow topping.

161

Chocolate ganache

MAKES: 2 | PREP TIME: 10 MINUTES | COOKING TIME: 2 MINUTES

INGREDIENTS

100 g / 3 ½ oz dark chocolate

350 ml / 11 ¾ fl. oz / 1 ½ cups double (heavy) cream

2 tbsp self-raising flour

1 tbsp cocoa

1 tbsp sugar sprinkles

METHOD

1. Break the chocolate into pieces and place into a heatproof bowl.

2. Pour 250 ml of the cream into a saucepan and gently heat until simmering. Pour over the chocolate and whisk until smooth and melted. Remove 1 tbsp for later.

3. Mix the flour and cocoa into the ganache to form a cake batter. Divide the batter between two mugs, transfer to a microwave and cook on full power for 2 minutes. Remove and set aside to cool.

4. Spoon the reserved chocolate around the rim of each mug. Whip the remaining cream until stiff and place on top of the cake before topping with the sprinkles.

Chocolate and strawberry

MAKES: 2 | PREP TIME: 10 MINUTES | COOKING TIME: 1 MINUTE, 30 SECONDS

INGREDIENTS

55 g / 2 oz / ¼ cup butter, softened

55 g / 2 oz / ¼ cup caster (superfine) sugar

1 large egg, beaten

55 g / 2 oz / ⅓ cup self-raising flour

1 tbsp cocoa

50 g / 1 ¾ oz / ½ cup strawberries

icing (confectioner's) sugar to dust

METHOD

1. In a mixing bowl, beat the butter and sugar together until pale and smooth. Add the egg to the bowl and mix through.

2. Sift the flour and cocoa into the bowl and fold through to form a batter.

3. Roughly chop the strawberries, reserving two as a garnish. Fold through the cake batter before dividing between two mugs.

4. Transfer to a microwave and cook on full power for 1 ½ minutes until a skewer inserted into the centre comes out clean. If not, return to the microwave for 15 seconds and test again.

5. Remove from the microwave and top with the reserved strawberries and dust with icing sugar.

163

Walnut mocha

MAKES: 2 | PREP TIME: 15 MINUTES | COOKING TIME: 1 MINUTE, 30 SECONDS

INGREDIENTS

55 g / 2 oz / ¼ cup butter, softened

55 g / 2 oz / ¼ cup caster (superfine) sugar

1 large egg

55 g / 2 oz / ⅓ cup self-raising flour, sifted

1 tsp instant espresso powder

1 tbsp unsweetened cocoa powder

1 tbsp walnuts, chopped

TO DECORATE

1 tbsp golden syrup

1 tbsp dark muscovado sugar

1 ½ tbsp butter

1 tsp unsweetened cocoa powder

1 tbsp walnuts, chopped

METHOD

1. Beat the butter and sugar together in a mug until pale and smooth.

2. Break the egg into a second mug and beat gently with a fork, then gradually stir into the butter mixture.

3. Fold in the flour, espresso powder, cocoa and walnuts. Divide the mixture between the two mugs and level the tops.

4. Transfer the mugs to a microwave and cook on full power for 1 ½ minutes until a skewer inserted into the centre comes out clean. If not, return to the microwave for 15 seconds and test again.

5. Create the topping by putting the golden syrup, muscovado sugar, butter and cocoa in a small bowl and microwaving for 20 seconds, stirring halfway through.

6. Spoon the sauce over the cakes and decorate with chopped walnuts. Leave to cool for 5 minutes before serving.

Gooey chocolate cream

MAKES: 2 | PREP TIME: 15 MINUTES | COOKING TIME: 1 MINUTE, 30 SECONDS

INGREDIENTS

55 g / 2 oz / ¼ cup butter, softened

55 g / 2 oz / ¼ cup caster (superfine) sugar

1 large egg, beaten

55 g / 2 oz / ⅓ cup self-raising flour, sifted

2 tbsp cocoa powder

2 chocolate truffles

TO DECORATE

125 ml / 4 ½ fl. oz / ½ cup double (heavy) cream

cocoa powder for sprinkling

METHOD

1. Beat the butter and sugar together in a mug until pale and smooth, then stir the egg into the mixture.

2. Fold in the flour and cocoa powder, then divide the mixture between two mugs. Press a chocolate truffle down into the centre of each cake and level the tops.

3. Transfer to a microwave and cook for 1 ½ minutes or until the cake is well risen.

4. Leave the cakes to cool for 10 minutes while you prepare the cream. Whip the cream with an electric whisk until it holds its shape, then spoon it into a piping bag fitted with a large star nozzle. Pipe a swirl of cream on top of each cake, then sprinkle with cocoa powder.

Marshmallow surprise

MAKES: 2 | PREP TIME: 15 MINUTES | COOKING TIME: 1 MINUTE, 30 SECONDS

INGREDIENTS

55 g / 2 oz / ¼ cup butter, softened

55 g / 2 oz / ¼ cup caster (superfine) sugar

1 large egg

½ tsp vanilla extract

55 g / 2 oz / ⅓ cup self-raising flour, sifted

2 tbsp mini marshmallows

TO DECORATE

30 g / 1 oz / ½ cup butter, softened

75 g / 2 ½ oz / ¾ cup icing (confectioner's) sugar,
plus extra for dusting

2–4 large marshmallow twirls

METHOD

1. Beat the butter and sugar together in a mug until pale and creamy.

2. Gently beat the egg in a second mug with the vanilla extract, then gradually stir into the butter mixture.

3. Fold in the flour and marshmallows, then divide the mixture between the two mugs and level the tops.

4. Transfer the mugs to a microwave and cook on full power for 1 ½ minutes until a skewer inserted into the centre comes out clean. If not, return to the microwave for 15 seconds and test again.

5. To decorate, beat the butter and icing sugar together until well whipped, adding a few drops of hot water if the mixture is too stiff.

6. Spoon the buttercream into a piping bag fitted with a large plain nozzle and pipe a big swirl on top of each cake. Stick a marshmallow twirl into the top of each swirl and dust lightly with icing sugar.

Cook's Corner

Mug Cakes

Toppings and accompaniments

Chocolate ice cream

SERVES: 4-6 | PREP TIME: 30 MINUTES

FREEZING TIME: 4 HOURS OR OVERNIGHT

INGREDIENTS

100 g / 3 ½ oz / ½ cup caster (superfine) sugar

100 ml / 3 ½ fl. oz / ½ cup water

150 g / 5 ¼ oz dark chocolate

500 ml / 17 fl. oz / 2 cups double (heavy) cream

2 tbsp pistachio nuts, chopped

2 tbsp chopped chocolate

METHOD

1. Place the sugar and water into a saucepan and heat enough to melt the sugar and create a syrup. Remove from the heat and set aside to cool.

2. Break the chocolate into pieces and place into a heatproof bowl suspended over some lightly simmering water, taking care that the bowl doesn't touch the water. Stir until the chocolate has melted, remove from the heat and set aside to cool.

3. Whip the cream until thickened and just about holding its shape. Fold the sugar syrup and melted chocolate through the whipped cream.

4. Place into a solid container and freezer for 1 hour. Remove and whisk the mixture together and place back into the freezer. Repeat this process every hour until the mixture is smooth, then place back into the freezer until firm, ideally overnight.

5. Remove from the freezer at least 30 minutes before serving to soften. Serve with the chopped nuts and chocolate on top.

Fudge

MAKES: 36 | PREP TIME: 15 MINUTES | COOKING TIME: 45 MINUTES

INGREDIENTS

300 ml / 10 ½ fl. oz / 1 ¼ cups whole milk

100 g / 3 ½ oz / ½ cup butter

350 g / 12 oz / 1 ½ cups caster (superfine) sugar

METHOD

1. Oil an 18 cm (7 in) square cake tin. Put the milk, butter and caster sugar in a large, heavy-based saucepan and stir over a low heat to dissolve the sugar. Increase the temperature a little and bring to the boil.

2. Boil the mixture for 35 minutes or until it reaches 115°C (240F) on a sugar thermometer, stirring constantly.

3. Remove the pan from the heat and continue to stir for 5 minutes.

4. Scrape the mixture into the prepared tin and level the surface with a palate knife. Leave to cool completely.

5. Turn the fudge out of the tin in one piece and cut into squares with a sharp knife.

6. Delicious grated on top of a mug cake or cut into small pieces and stirred into your cake mixture before baking.

Classic buttercream

MAKES: 200 ML | PREPARATION TIME: 5 MINUTES

INGREDIENTS

100 g / 3 ½ oz / ½ cup butter, softened

200 g / 7 oz / 2 cups icing (confectioner's) sugar

1 tsp vanilla extract

METHOD

1. Beat the butter until smooth with an electric whisk.

2. Gradually incorporate the icing sugar, whisking all the time, until smooth.

3. Whisk in the vanilla extract and add a few drops of hot water if necessary to reach your desired consistency.

4. Spoon or pipe on top of your mug cakes.

176

Strawberry yogurt icing

MAKES: 1 BOWL | PREP TIME: 10 MINUTES | CHILLING TIME: 30 MINUTES

••••••••••••••••••••••••

INGREDIENTS

100 g / 3 ½ oz strawberries

500 g / 1 lb 1 oz natural yogurt

100 g / 3 ½ oz / 1 cup icing (confectioner's) sugar

METHOD

1. Wash the strawberries before dehulling and cutting in half.

2. Place into a blender and blend for 2-3 minutes until smooth.

3. Pass the blended strawberries a sieve into the yogurt.

4. Whisk the yogurt together with the icing sugar until thick and glossy.

5. Place into the refrigerator for 30 minutes to firm at which point it will be ready to use.

177

Chocolate dipped strawberries

MAKES: 20 | PREP TIME: 10 MINUTES | CHILLING TIME: 30 MINUTES

INGREDIENTS

20 whole strawberries

150 g / 5 ¼ oz dark chocolate

METHOD

1. Line a baking tray with greaseproof paper.

2. Wash the strawberries and pat dry with kitchen paper.

3. Break the chocolate into a heatproof bowl and place over a pan of simmering water, ensuring the bowl does not touch the water. Stir until melted and smooth, then turn off the heat under the pan.

4. Dip each of the strawberries into the melted chocolate, allowing any excess chocolate to drip back into the bowl, then place on the baking tray.

5. Once they have all been dipped, move the tray to a refrigerator for 30 minutes until set and firm.

Vanilla custard

MAKES: 600 ML | PREP TIME: 25 MINUTES | COOKING TIME: 10 MINUTES

INGREDIENTS

450 ml / 12 ½ fl. oz / 1 ¾ cups whole milk

1 vanilla pod, split lengthways

4 large egg yolks

75 g / 2 ½ oz / ⅓ cup caster (superfine) sugar

METHOD

1. Combine the milk and vanilla pod in a saucepan and bring to simmering point, then turn off the heat and leave to infuse for 20 minutes.

2. Whisk the egg yolks with the caster sugar until thick.

3. Gradually incorporate the hot milk, whisking all the time, then scrape the mixture back into the saucepan.

4. Stir the custard over a low heat until it just starts to thicken, then put the base of the pan in cold water and continue to stir until the custard cools a little and the danger of curdling has passed. Serve warm.

Dark hot chocolate sauce

MAKES: 200 ML | PREP TIME: 5 MINUTES | COOKING TIME: 5 MINUTES

INGREDIENTS

100 ml / 3 ½ fl. oz / ½ cup double (heavy) cream

1 tbsp runny honey

1 tbsp brandy

100 g / 3 ½ oz / ⅔ cup dark chocolate
(minimum 70% cocoa solids), chopped

METHOD

1. Put the cream, honey and brandy in a small
   saucepan and heat to simmering point.

2. Put the chopped chocolate in a heatproof
   bowl and pour over the cream.

3. Wait for 30 seconds, then stir gently
   until emulsified.

4. Immediately spoon over your mug cakes.

Salted caramel spread

MAKES: 350 G | PREP TIME: 5 MINUTES | COOKING TIME: 10 MINUTES

INGREDIENTS

100 g / 3 ½ oz / ½ cup butter

100 g / 3 ½ oz / ½ cup muscovado sugar

100 g / 3 ½ oz / ⅓ cup golden syrup

50 ml / 1 ¾ fl. oz / ¼ cup double (heavy) cream

½ tsp sea salt

METHOD

1. Put all of the ingredients in a small saucepan and stir over a low heat until the sugar dissolves.

2. Increase the heat to medium and simmer for 4 minutes, stirring occasionally.

3. Pour the sauce into a sterilised jar and leave to cool.

4. Store the caramel spread in the fridge before using.

5. Swirl into your mug cake mixture before cooking for added flavour or spoon on top of a cooked mug cake for decoration.

181

Fudge brownie cookies

MAKES: 12-16 | PREP TIME: 30 MINUTES | COOKING TIME: 15 MINUTES

INGREDIENTS

100 g / 3 ½ oz dark chocolate

100 g / 3 ½ oz / ½ cup unsalted butter

200 g / 7 oz / ¾ cup caster (superfine) sugar

2 free range eggs, lightly whisked

1 tsp vanilla extract

150 g / 5 ¼ oz / 1 ½ cups ground almonds

50 g / 1 ¾ oz / ½ cup cocoa powder

2 tsp baking powder

a pinch of salt

METHOD

1. Preheat the oven to 180°C (160°C fan) / 350F / gas 4 and line a baking tray with greaseproof paper.

2. Break the chocolate into pieces and melt gently with the butter in a heatproof bowl over simmering water, taking care that the water does not touch the bowl. Remove from the heat and allow to cool.

3. Whisk together the sugar, eggs and vanilla extract until pale and doubled in size.

4. Fold the cooled chocolate mixture into the eggs followed by the ground almonds, cocoa powder, baking powder and salt. Mix until all the ingredients are combined.

5. Chill the mixture in the fridge for 20 minutes to firm up.

6. Roll the dough into balls and place onto the baking tray before lightly squashing down. You may need a second tray or to cook them in batches.

7. Place into the oven and cook for 12-15 minutes until crisp on the outside but still gooey inside, then remove to cool on a wire rack.

Coconut ice cream

SERVES: 4-6 | COOKING TIME: 30 MINUTES
FREEZING TIME: 4 HOURS OR OVERNIGHT

● ●

INGREDIENTS

4 egg yolks

200 g / 7 oz / ¾ cup caster (superfine) sugar

2 vanilla pod

250 ml / 9 fl. oz / 1 cup double (heavy) cream

250 ml / 9 fl. oz / 1 cup coconut milk

100 g / 3 ½ oz / 1 cup desiccated coconut

METHOD

1. Whisk the egg yolks and sugar together until pale and creamy.

2. Halve the vanilla pods and scrape out the seeds. Place the vanilla pods, cream and coconut milk into a saucepan and gently heat until just starting to bubble.

3. Remove the vanilla pods and slowly pour over the egg yolks whilst whisking continuously. Pour through a sieve back into the saucepan and add the vanilla seeds and desiccated coconut to the pan. Cover and leave to cool completely.

4. Pour the cooled mixture into a freezer-proof container and freeze for 4 hours or overnight until firm.

Zabaglione

SERVES: 4 | PREP TIME: 5 MINUTES | COOKING TIME: 10 MINUTES

INGREDIENTS

3 large egg yolks

2 ½ tbsp caster (superfine) sugar

2 ½ tbsp Marsala

METHOD

1. Set a heatproof bowl over a saucepan of simmering water, making sure the bottom of the bowl does not come into contact with the water.

2. Add the egg yolks, sugar and Marsala to the bowl and whisk vigorously until the mixture thickens.

3. The zabaglione is ready when you can drizzle a line of the mixture off the whisk back into the bowl and the trail stays visible for a few seconds.

4. Remove the bowl from the saucepan and serve immediately.

Cinnamon caramel sauce

MAKES: 400 ML | PREP TIME: 15 MINUTES | COOKING TIME: 8 MINUTES

INGREDIENTS

100 ml / 3 ½ fl. oz / ½ cup double (heavy) cream

100 g / 3 ½ oz / ½ cup butter

100 g / 3 ½ oz / ⅓ cup golden syrup

100 g / 3 ½ oz / ½ cup muscovado sugar

1 tsp ground cinnamon

METHOD

1. Put all of the ingredients in a small saucepan and stir over a low heat until the sugar dissolves.

2. Increase the heat to medium and simmer for 2 minutes, stirring occasionally.

3. Leave the sauce to cool for 10 minutes before serving warm, spooned over your mug cakes.

Vanilla ice cream

SERVES: 4-6 | PREP TIME: 30 MINUTES
COOKING TIME: 4 HOURS OR OVERNIGHT

INGREDIENTS

4 egg yolks

200 g / 7 oz / ¾ cup caster (superfine) sugar

2 vanilla pod

500 ml / 17 fl. oz / 2 cups double (heavy) cream

METHOD

1. Whisk the egg yolks and sugar together until pale and creamy.

2. Halve the vanilla pods and scrape out the seeds. Place the vanilla pods and cream into a saucepan and gently heat until just starting to bubble.

3. Remove the vanilla pods from the cream and slowly pour over the egg yolks whilst whisking continuously. Pour through a sieve back into the saucepan and add the vanilla seeds to the pan. Cover and leave to cool completely.

4. Pour into a freezer-proof container and freeze for 4 hours or overnight until firm.

Avocado and spinach ice cream

SERVES: 4-6 | PREP TIME: 20 MINUTES

COOKING TIME: 4 HOURS OR OVERNIGHT

INGREDIENTS

500 ml / 17 fl. oz / 2 cups coconut milk

2 ripe avocados, peeled and chopped

50 g / 1 ¾ oz / ½ cup spinach, washed

1 lime, zest and juice

1 tsp vanilla extract

2 tbsp honey

METHOD

1. Add the coconut milk to a blender along with the rest of the ingredients. Blend for 1-2 minutes until smooth.

2. Transfer the mixture to an ice cream maker and churn for 1 hour until ready.

3. Place the ice cream into a freezer-proof container and freeze for 4 hours or overnight until firm.

Mini meringues

MAKES: 24 | PREP TIME: 20 MINUTES | COOKING TIME: 1 HOUR

INGREDIENTS

4 large egg whites

100 g / 3 ½ oz / ½ cup caster (superfine) sugar

METHOD

1. Preheat the oven to 140°C (120°C fan) / 275F / gas 1 and oil and line a large baking tray with greaseproof paper.

2. Whisk the egg whites with an electric whisk until stiff, then gradually whisk in half the caster sugar until very shiny. Fold in the remaining sugar, being careful to retain as much air as possible.

3. Spoon into a piping bag fitted with a large star nozzle and pipe small rosettes onto the tray.

4. Transfer the tray to the oven and bake for 1 hour. Turn off the oven and leave the meringues to cool slowly inside before serving whole or crumbled on top of your mug cakes.

189

Marmalade

MAKES: 4 JARS | PREP TIME: 10 MINUTES
COOKING TIME: 2 HOURS, 30 MINUTES

INGREDIENTS

4 oranges

1 lemon

2 l / 68 fl. oz / 8 cups water

1 kg jam (jelly) sugar

METHOD

1. Wash the oranges and lemon before placing into a pan with the water and boiling for up to 2 hours or until very soft.

2. Remove the fruits with a slotted spoon. Once cool enough to handle cut into wedges and remove the pips.

3. Squeeze the juice from the fruit in to the water before thinly slicing the fruit and returning to the pan.

4. Add the sugar and heat until boiling and the sugar has dissolved. Cook for 12-15 minutes before checking it is ready by spooning some onto a chilled plate. If it sets on the plate and wrinkles when pushed with your finger it is ready.

5. Turn off the heat to settle for 15 minutes before spooning into sterilising jars and covering with a disc of greaseproof paper before replacing the lid.

Vanilla shortbread

MAKES: 16 | PREP TIME: 45 MINUTES | COOKING TIME: 20 MINUTES

INGREDIENTS

300 g / 10 ½ oz / 2 cups plain (all-purpose) flour

200 g / 7 oz / ¾ cup unsalted butter, chilled

125 g / 4 ¼ oz / ½ cup caster (superfine) sugar

2 tsp vanilla extract

2 free range egg yolks

METHOD

1. Place the flour into a mixing bowl and add the butter cut into cubes. Rub in using your fingertips until it resembles breadcrumbs.

2. Stir the sugar through the mixture before adding the vanilla and egg yolks.

3. Mix together using a fork until a dough starts to form. Once this happens bring together with your hands and turn out onto a lightly floured surface and knead enough to form a smooth dough.

4. Roll out the dough to the desired thickness and cut out rounds using a pastry cutter. Place onto a baking tray lined with greaseproof paper and place into the refrigerator for at least 30 minutes.

5. Preheat the oven to 180°C (160°C fan) / 350F / gas 4.

6. Place the biscuits into the oven and cook for 18-20 minutes until golden and crisp.

7. Remove and set aside to cool completely.

Caramel popcorn

MAKES: 1-2 | PREP TIME: 10 MINUTES | COOKING TIME: 30 MINUTES

INGREDIENTS

1 tbsp sunflower oil

75 g / 2 ½ oz popping corn

100 g / 3 ½ oz / ½ cup salted butter

200 g / 7 oz / 1 ¼ cups soft brown sugar

½ tsp bicarbonate of (baking) soda

½ tsp vanilla extract

METHOD

1. Preheat the oven to 140°C (120°C fan) / 275F / gas 1.

2. Heat the oil in a large saucepan over a medium high heat. Add the corn and swirl around in the oil, cover with the lid and turn the heat to low. Cook until the popping stops; shake occasionally.

3. Heat the butter in a separate saucepan over a medium heat. Stir the sugar into the butter until it dissolves, then leave to bubble for 3-5 minutes but do not boil. Remove from the heat and quickly whisk in the bicarbonate of soda and vanilla extract.

4. Pour the caramel sauce over the popped corn and toss to coat. Turn out onto a baking tray and place into the oven for 12-15 minutes until crisp, stirring occasionally to cook evenly.

Chocolate banana pops

MAKES: 8-10 | PREP TIME: 2 HOURS

INGREDIENTS

3 bananas

150 g / 5 ¼ oz dark chocolate

75 g / 2 ½ oz / ⅔ cup chopped hazelnuts

METHOD

1. Peel and chop the bananas into good sized pieces and insert a skewer into each piece. Place the pieces in a food bag and into the freezer for up to an hour to firm up.

2. Break the chocolate into a heatproof bowl and place over a pan of simmering water, ensuring the bowl does not touch the water. Stir until melted and smooth, then turn off the heat.

3. Dip the frozen bananas into the melted chocolate, allowing any excess chocolate to drip back into the bowl.

4. Roll in the hazelnuts as desired, then place onto a baking tray covered with greaseproof paper. Place into the refrigerator for 1 hour to set.

Blueberry ice cream

SERVES: 4-6 | PREP TIME: 30 MINUTES
FREEZING TIME: 4 HOURS OR OVERNIGHT

INGREDIENTS

1 lemon, juice and zest

150 g / 5 ¼ oz / ⅔ cup caster (superfine) sugar

150 g / 5 ¼ oz / 1 cup blueberries, plus more to serve

500 ml / 17 fl. oz / 2 cups double (heavy) cream

METHOD

1. Combine the lemon, caster sugar and blueberries in a saucepan and heat gently until the sugar has dissolved and the berries start to break down. Place into a blender and blend until smooth. Leave to cool.

2. Whip the cream until just holding its shape, then fold through the mixture to combine.

3. Move into a suitable container and freeze for 1 hour. Remove and whisk the mixture, then return to the freezer. Repeat every hour until smooth, then freeze until firm or overnight.

4. Remove from the freezer for 30 minutes, before serving with fresh blueberries.

Mixed berry jam

MAKES: 700 ML | PREP TIME: 15 MINUTES | COOKING TIME: 40 MINUTES

INGREDIENTS

450 g / 1 lb / 2 cups granulated sugar

450 g / 1 lb / 3 cups raspberries, strawberries and blueberries

1 lemon, juiced

METHOD

1. Preheat the oven to 110°C (90° fan) / 225F / gas ¼.

2. Put the sugar in a heatproof bowl and transfer it to the oven along with two glass jars while you start cooking the fruit.

3. Put the berries and lemon juice in a large saucepan and cover. Heat gently for 10 minutes or until they soften in the juice they produce.

4. Stir in the warmed sugar until it dissolves, then increase the heat and boil until the mixture reads 107°C (225F) on a sugar thermometer.

5. Leave to cool and thicken for 10 minutes, then ladle into the prepared jars and seal with clean lids or waxed paper.

197

Strawberry and vanilla marshmallows

MAKES: 25 | PREP TIME: 45 MINUTES | COOKING TIME: 10 MINUTES

SETTING TIME: 2 HOURS

INGREDIENTS

2 tbsp cornflour (cornstarch)

8 gelatine leaves

250 g / 9 oz / 1 ¼ cups caster (superfine) sugar

1 vanilla pod, seeds only

50 ml / 1 ¾ fl. oz / ¼ cup strawberry syrup

1 large egg white

25 g / 1 oz / ¼ cup icing (confectioner's) sugar

METHOD

1. Oil an 18 cm (7 inch) square cake tin and dust it with cornflour. Put the gelatine leaves in a shallow bowl and cover them with 50 ml of cold water.

2. Put the caster sugar in a small saucepan with 135 ml of cold water then stir over a low heat until the sugar has dissolved. Increase the heat and let the mixture boil without stirring until it reaches 120°C (248F) on a sugar thermometer. Take the pan off the heat and carefully stir in the gelatine with its soaking water, the vanilla seeds and strawberry syrup.

3. Whisk the egg whites in a freestanding mixer until they form stiff peaks, then pour in the gelatine syrup in a thin stream with the whisk still running. Continue to whisk for 10 minutes on high speed while the marshmallow cools.

4. Scrape the mixture into the tin and level the top, then leave to set for 2 hours. Turn the marshmallow out of the tin onto a work surface that has been dusted with icing sugar. Dip a sharp knife into hot water, then cut the marshmallow into cubes, cleaning and re-dipping the knife as necessary.

Chocolate fudge

MAKES: 36 | PREP TIME: 5 MINUTES | COOKING TIME: 10 MINUTES

CHILLING TIME: 1 HOUR

INGREDIENTS

400 g / 14 oz dark chocolate

400 g / 14 oz condensed milk

50 g / 1 ¾ oz / ¼ cup butter

100 g / 3 ½ oz / 1 cup icing (confectioner's) sugar

METHOD

1. Break up the chocolate and place into a saucepan with the condensed milk and butter. Heat gently until the contents have melted and mix together.

2. Remove from the heat and sift the icing sugar into the melted chocolate. Whisk thoroughly until fully combined and the mixture has stiffened.

3. Pour into a square cake tin lined with greaseproof paper. Spread evenly to cover the entire base of the tin.

4. Place into the refrigerator for at least 1 hour until firm. Remove and cut into squares using a sharp knife.

5. Store in an airtight container for up to one week.

Nutty dulce de leche

MAKES: 450 G | PREP TIME: 5 MINUTES | COOKING TIME: 3 HOURS
CHILLING TIME: 2 HOURS

INGREDIENTS

1 x 400 g / 14 oz can sweetened condensed milk, unopened

50 g / 1 ¾ oz / ½ cup hazelnuts, chopped

25 g / 1 oz / ¼ cup almonds, chopped

METHOD

1. Put the unopened can of condensed milk in a saucepan of water and simmer for 3 hours. Check the water level occasionally to ensure it doesn't boil dry.

2. Leave the can to cool completely before opening.

3. Spoon the dulce de leche into a bowl and beat until smooth. Fold in two thirds of the nuts, then sprinkle the rest on top.

4. Spoon on top of your mug cakes for extra flavour.

Vanilla berry swirl ice cream

SERVES: 4-6 | PREP TIME: 30 MINUTES

FREEZING TIME: 4 HOURS OR OVERNIGHT

INGREDIENTS

4 egg yolks

200 g / 7 oz / ¾ cup caster (superfine) sugar

2 vanilla pods

500 ml / 17 fl. oz / 2 cups double (heavy) cream

300 g / 10 ½ oz / 2 cups mixed frozen berries

METHOD

1. Whisk the egg yolks and sugar together.

2. Halve the vanilla pods and remove the seeds. Gently heat the pods and cream in a pan until just starting to bubble, then remove the pods and slowly whisk into the egg yolks.

3. Pour through a sieve back into the saucepan and add the vanilla seeds to the pan. Cover and leave to cool completely.

4. Blend the berries in a blender until smooth. Pass through a sieve and collect in a bowl.

5. Pour the cooled mixture into a freezer-proof container before swirling through the berry purée. Freeze until firm or overnight.

Pink meringue kisses

MAKES: 20 | PREP TIME: 20 MINUTES | COOKING TIME: 45 MINUTES

INGREDIENTS

4 egg whites

120 g / 4 ¼ oz / ½ cup caster (superfine) sugar

120 g / 4 ¼ oz / 1 ¼ cups icing (confectioner's) sugar

1 tsp pink food dye

METHOD

1. Preheat the oven to 140°C (120°C fan) / 275F / gas 1 and line two baking trays with parchment paper.

2. In a bowl, whisk the egg whites until soft peaks form. Gradually add the caster sugar whilst continuing to whisk until stiff peaks form and the egg whites have become glossy.

3. Sift a third of the icing sugar into the bowl and gently fold through, repeat this twice more until the mixture is soft and billowy, then gently fold through the food dye.

4. Spoon into a piping bag fitted with a star nozzle and pipe onto the baking trays at regular intervals, leaving space between each to spread.

5. Bake in the oven for 45 minutes until crisp, then remove to cool before carefully removing.

Crunchy chocolate chip cookies

MAKES: 16 | PREP TIME: 20 MINUTES | COOKING TIME: 18 MINUTES

INGREDIENTS

225 g / 8 oz / 1 ½ cups plain (all-purpose) flour

75 g / 2 ½ oz / ⅓ cup caster (superfine) sugar

150 g / 5 oz / ⅔ cup butter, cubed

50 g / 1 ¾ oz / ¼ cup chocolate chips

METHOD

1. Preheat the oven to 180°C (160°C fan) / 350F / gas 4 and line a baking tray with greaseproof paper.

2. Mix together the flour and caster sugar in a bowl, then rub in the butter. Knead gently with the chocolate chips until a smooth dough forms, then divide it into 16 pieces.

3. Roll each piece of dough into a ball, then press it onto the baking tray.

4. Bake the cookies for 18 minutes, turning the tray round halfway through. Transfer the cookies to a wire rack and leave to cool.

5. Crumble on top of your mug cakes or mix into the cake mixture for added crunch.

Cherry jam

MAKES: 1 POT | PREP TIME: 10 MINUTES | COOKING TIME: 40 MINUTES

INGREDIENTS

500 g / 1 lb 1 oz fresh cherries

½ lemon, juiced

50 ml / 1 ¾ fl. oz / ¼ cup water

500 g / 1 lb 1 oz / 2 ¼ cups caster (superfine) sugar

25 g / 1 oz / ¼ cup unsalted butter

METHOD

1. Wash the cherries, remove the stalks and cut in half to remove the stone. Place into a saucepan with the lemon juice and water.

2. Heat to a boil, reduce the heat to a simmer and leave for 15 minutes to soften. Remove from the heat and stir the sugar into the pan until it has dissolved.

3. Return to the heat and mix through the butter. Increase the heat and boil for 15 minutes.

4. It is ready if a spoonful of jam placed onto a chilled plate sets and the surface wrinkles when pushed with your finger. Pour into a clean, sterilized jar and cover immediately.

Chocolate meringues

MAKES: 20 | PREP TIME: 20 MINUTES | COOKING TIME: 45 MINUTES

INGREDIENTS

3 egg whites

150 g / 5 ¼ oz / ⅔ cup caster (superfine) sugar

50 g / 1 ¾ oz dark chocolate, finely grated

1 tbsp cocoa

METHOD

1. Preheat the oven to 140°C (120°C fan) / 275F / gas 1 and line two baking trays with greaseproof paper.

2. In a clean bowl, whisk the egg whites until soft peaks form.

3. Gradually whisk the sugar into the egg whites until stiff peaks form and they become glossy.

4. Mix together the chocolate and cocoa before folding into the egg whites.

5. Spoon into a piping bag and pipe onto the baking trays at regular intervals, leaving space between each to spread.

6. Bake in the oven for 40-45 minutes until crisp. Remove to cool before removing carefully.

Apple caramel sauce

MAKES: 1 JAR | PREP TIME: 10 MINUTES | COOKING TIME: 20 MINUTES

INGREDIENTS

2 apples

100 g / 3 ½ oz / ½ cup butter

200 g / 7 oz / 1 ¼ cups soft brown sugar

1 tbsp golden syrup

150 ml / 5 ¼ fl. oz / ⅔ cup double (heavy) cream

METHOD

1. Peel and core the apples before chopping into cubes. Place into a saucepan with a small amount of water and heat until boiling to break down. As they soften, use a wooden spoon to break them down to a purée.

2. Add the butter to the pan followed by the sugar and syrup. Heat until bubbling and the sugar dissolves, taking care not to boil. Stir to combine and bubble for 3-5 minutes.

3. Pour the cream into the pan and mix through until the colour lightens. Heat through for a further 2-3 minutes until combined and smooth.

4. Remove from the heat to cool a little before pouring into a jar or other container.

Walnut fudge

MAKES: 36 | COOKING TIME: 20 MINUTES | CHILLING TIME: 1 HOUR

INGREDIENTS

500 g / 1 lb 1 oz / 2 ¾ cups dark soft brown sugar

200 ml / 7 fl. oz / ¾ cup condensed milk

50 g / 1 ¾ oz / ¼ cup butter

1 tsp vanilla extract

75 g / 2 ½ oz walnut halves

METHOD

1. Gently heat the sugar and condensed milk in a saucepan until the sugar has melted and the temperature reaches 115°C.

2. Remove from the heat and stir through the butter and vanilla extract. Beat the mixture with a wooden spoon until no longer glossy.

3. Roughly chop the nuts, reserving some for the topping. Fold through the mixture, then pour into a square tin lined with greaseproof paper. Spread evenly before topping with the reserved nuts.

4. Place into the refrigerator for 1 hour until set. Remove and cut into squares with a sharp knife. Store in an airtight container for up to 1 week.

Meringue clouds

MAKES: 20 | PREP TIME: 20 MINUTES | COOKING TIME: 45 MINUTES

INGREDIENTS

4 egg whites

120 g / 4 ¼ oz / ½ cup caster (superfine) sugar

120 g / 4 ¼ oz / 1 ¼ cups icing (confectioner's) sugar

50 g / 1 ¾ oz / ½ cup whipped cream

METHOD

1. Preheat the oven to 140°C (120°C fan) / 275F / gas 1 and line two baking trays with greaseproof paper.

2. In a clean non-plastic bowl, whisk the egg whites until soft peaks form. Gradually whisk the caster sugar into the whites until stiff peaks form and they become glossy.

3. Sift a third of the icing sugar into the bowl and gently fold through, repeat this twice more until the mixture is soft and billowy.

4. Spoon into a piping bag and pipe onto the baking trays at regular intervals leaving space between each to spread.

5. Bake in the oven for 40-45 minutes until crisp. Remove to cool before carefully removing using a palette knife.

6. Place a small amount of cream onto the base of a meringue before sticking a second to it. Repeat until all the meringues have been used.

7. Insert a cocktail stick as desired or use to top a cake.

Apricot jam

MAKES: 1 POT | PREP TIME: 10 MINUTES | COOKING TIME: 40 MINUTES

INGREDIENTS

300 g / 10 ½ oz apricots, halved

½ lemon, juiced

100 ml / 3 ½ fl. oz / ½ cup water

300 g / 10 ½ oz / 1 ⅓ cups caster (superfine) sugar

1 tbsp unsalted butter

METHOD

1. Place the apricots into a pan with the lemon juice and water. Heat until boiling, then reduce to a simmer and leave for 15 minutes to soften.

2. Remove from the heat and stir the sugar into the pan until it has dissolved.

3. Return to the heat and mix through the butter. Increase the heat to a boil and leave for a further 15 minutes.

4. It is ready if a spoonful of jam placed onto a chilled plate sets and the surface wrinkles when pushed with your finger.

5. Pour into a clean sterilised jar and cover immediately.

Strawberry sorbet

SERVES: 6-8 | PREP TIME: 20 MINUTES
CHILLING TIME: 4 HOURS OR OVERNIGHT

INGREDIENTS

200 g / 7 oz / ¾ cup caster (superfine) sugar

2 limes, juiced

200 ml / 7 fl. oz / ¾ cup water

500 g / 1 lb 1 oz strawberries

METHOD

1. Heat the sugar, lime juice and water over a medium heat in a saucepan. Stir until the sugar has dissolved and you have a syrup. Remove from the heat and set aside to cool.

2. Wash the strawberries before dehulling and cutting in half. Place into a blender and blend for 2-3 minutes until smooth.

3. Pass the strawberries through a sieve into the syrup. Pour into a shallow metal container and place in the freezer. Leave for 30 minutes until ice crystals have formed at the edges. Stir the edges into the centre and return to the freezer. Repeat every 20 minutes until frozen.

4. Place into an airtight container and freeze for 4 hours or overnight.

Chocolate hazelnut spread

MAKES: 660 G | PREP TIME: 15 MINUTES | COOKING TIME: 5 MINUTES

INGREDIENTS

200 ml / 7 fl. oz / ¾ cup double (heavy) cream

150 g / 5 ½ oz / 1 cup dark chocolate,
(minimum 70% cocoa solids), chopped

150 g / 5 ½ oz / 1 cup milk chocolate, chopped

200 g / 7 oz / 1 ⅔ cups roasted hazelnuts, skinned

2 tbsp hazelnut oil (or sunflower if unavailable)

2 tbsp icing (confectioner's) sugar

METHOD

1. Heat the cream until it starts to simmer, then pour it over the chopped chocolate and leave to stand for 30 seconds. Stir gently together until just combined.

2. Put the hazelnuts in a liquidizer with the oil and icing sugar. Grind to an oily paste, pausing to scrape down the sides occasionally.

3. Scrape the chocolate mixture into the liquidizer and blend again until very smooth.

4. Scrape into a bowl or jar and leave to cool completely before serving spooned on top of your mug cakes.

214

Mint chocolate buttercream

MAKES: 250 ML | PREPARATION TIME: 5 MINUTES

INGREDIENTS

100 g / 3 ½ oz / ½ cup butter, softened

200 g / 7 oz / 2 cups icing (confectioner's) sugar

2 tbsp unsweetened cocoa powder

1 tbsp whole milk

a few drops peppermint extract

METHOD

1. Beat the butter until smooth with an electric whisk.

2. Gradually incorporate the icing sugar, whisking all the time, until smooth.

3. Stir the cocoa powder, milk and peppermint extract together, then whisk the mixture into the buttercream.

4. Spoon or pipe the buttercream on top of your mug cakes for extra indulgence and flavour.

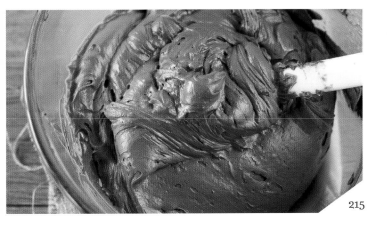

215

Blueberry yogurt ice cream

SERVES: 4-6 | PREP TIME: 10 MINUTES

FREEZING TIME: 4 HOURS OR OVERNIGHT

INGREDIENTS

500 g / 1 lb 1 oz frozen blueberries

500 g / 1 lb 1 oz Greek yogurt

2 tbsp honey

50 g / 1 ¾ oz / ½ cup fresh blueberries

METHOD

1. Place the frozen berries, yogurt and honey in a blender. Blend together for 1 minute until combined, then spoon into a bowl.

2. Fold the fresh berries into the yogurt mixture.

3. Place into an ice cream maker and process as per the manufacturers' guidelines. Alternatively, move into a suitable container and freeze for 1 hour. Remove and whisk the mixture, then return to the freezer. Repeat every hour until smooth.

4. Once ready, place into the freezer for 4 hours or overnight to set fully.

Plum jam

MAKES: 1 POT | PREP TIME: 10 MINUTES | COOKING TIME: 40 MINUTES

INGREDIENTS

500 g / 1 lb 1 oz plums

½ lemon, juiced

50 ml / 1 ¾ fl. oz / ¼ cup water

500 g / 1 lb 1 oz / 2 ¼ cups caster (superfine) sugar

25 g / 1 oz / ¼ cup unsalted butter

METHOD

1. Wash the plums, remove the stalks and cut in half to remove the stone.

2. Heat in a saucepan with the lemon juice and water until boiling, then reduce the heat to a simmer and leave for 15 minutes to soften.

3. Remove from the heat and stir the sugar into the pan until it has dissolved. Return to the heat and mix through the butter. Increase the heat and leave to boil for a further 15 minutes.

4. It is ready if a spoonful of jam placed onto a chilled plate sets and the surface wrinkles when pushed with your finger. Pour into a clean sterilised jar and cover immediately.

Raspberry macarons

MAKES: 18-20 | PREP TIME: 30 MINUTES | COOKING TIME: 15 MINUTES

INGREDIENTS

50 g / 1 ¾ oz / ½ cup raspberries

100 g / 3 ½ oz / 1 cup ground almonds

100 g / 3 ½ oz / 1 cup icing (confectioner's) sugar

3 egg whites

100 g / 3 ½ oz / ½ cup caster (superfine) sugar

150 ml / 5 ¼ fl. oz / ⅔ cup double (heavy) cream, whipped

METHOD

1. Place the raspberries into a blender and blend until smooth. Pass through a sieve into a bowl and set aside.

2. Place the ground almonds and icing sugar into a bowl and whisk together to combine. Add one of the egg whites and set aside without mixing.

3. Place the remaining egg whites into a metallic bowl and start to whisk until soft peaks form.

4. At the same time, place the sugar into a saucepan with a splash of water and heat until the sugar dissolves and a sugar thermometer reads 121°C. Slowly pour the syrup into the egg whites whilst continuing to whisk on high speed for three minutes.

5. Fold the whisked egg whites into the almond mixture until thick and glossy, adding the raspberry purée as you do so.

6. Preheat the oven to 160°C (140°C fan) / 325F / gas 3 and line a baking tray with greaseproof paper.

7. Spoon the macaron mixture into a piping bag and pipe circles onto the baking tray at regular intervals. Place into the refrigerator for 20 minutes to chill before placing into the oven for 12-15 minutes.

8. Remove from the oven and allow to cool completely before carefully removing. Stick the cooled macarons together with some whipped cream in between.

Cocoa ripple meringues

MAKES: 10 | PREP TIME: 30 MINUTES | COOKING TIME: 1 HOUR

INGREDIENTS

100 g / 3 ½ oz / ½ cup caster (superfine) sugar

4 large egg whites

¼ tsp cream of tartar

2 tbsp unsweetened cocoa powder

METHOD

1. Preheat the oven to 200°C (180°C fan) / 400F / gas 6 and line a large baking tray with greaseproof paper.

2. Spread the sugar out on the baking tray and heat in the oven for 8 minutes. Meanwhile, whisk the egg whites and cream of tartar in a freestanding mixer until stiff.

3. When the sugar is ready, remove it from the oven and reduce the temperature to 140°C (120°C fan) / 275F / gas 1. Pour the hot sugar in a slow continuous stream into the egg whites, whisking all the time. Continue to whisk on high speed for 10 minutes or until the side of the bowl feels cold.

4. Sieve the cocoa powder over the top, then fold and ripple it through with a large metal spoon. Space out heaped spoonfuls of the meringue on the baking tray.

5. Transfer the tray to the oven and bake for 1 hour. Turn off the oven and leave the meringues to cool slowly inside before serving.

6. Delicious crumbled over the top of mug cakes.

INDEX